DOUBLE AGENT

DOUBLE AGENT

MY SECRET LIFE
UNDERCOVER IN THE IRA

KEVIN FULTON

WITH JIM NALLY AND
IAN GALLAGHER

JOHN BLAKE

Published by John Blake Publishing,
The Plaza,
535 Kings Road,
Chelsea Harbour,
London SW10 0SZ

www.facebook.com/johnblakebooks 🖪
twitter.com/jblakebooks 🅴

First published in hardback by John Blake Publishing in 2006 as *Unsung Hero*.
First published in paperback in 2008.
This paperback edition first published in 2019.

Paperback ISBN: 978 1 78946 134 3
Ebook ISBN: 987 1 78946 200 5

British Library Cataloguing-in-Publication Data:

A catalogue record for this book is available from the British Library.

Design by www.envydesign.co.uk

Printed and bound in Great Britain by Clays Ltd, Elcograf S.p.A.

1 3 5 7 9 10 8 6 4 2

John Blake Publishing is an imprint of Bonnier Books UK
www.bonnierbooks.co.uk

KEVIN FULTON was brought up in Newry, County Down in Northern Ireland. At 18 he became a British soldier and was soon recruited to be an agent. He infiltrated the terrorist organisation and remained there for 15 years, supplying inside information to the security forces. So integrated was he, even his wife and family believed that he was working for the Provos. Abandoned by his military chiefs when he most needed them, Fulton fled to Northern Ireland in 1994, lying low in England and Thailand. He returned to Northern Ireland in 1997, when the ceasefire seemed to hold.

JIM NALLY is a documentary producer and director for the BBC, Channel 4 and Channel 5. Before that he was a free lance writer for a number of Fleet Street newspapers.

IAN GALLAGHER has been a national newspaper journalist fro the past 15 years and has covered the conflicts in Kosovo and Afghanistan.

ACKNOWLEDGEMENTS

I would like to thank Nic Robertson and Henry Schuster of CNN, Trevor Birney of UTV, Chris Anderson, Liam Clarke of the *Sunday Times* and Kathryn Johnston, Neil Mackay, Greg Harkin, Martin Ingram, Stephen Dempster, Hugh Jordan, Tommy, Mark Birdsall, Jane Winter, also Jock and Gerry, Jim and Henry. Thanks also to Toli and Carol for their help and friendship over the last few years.

Most of all, I would like to thank all former and serving members of the security forces who assisted me with this book, but who I cannot name in case they lose their pensions. Thank you, each and every one of you, for your help and support over the years. Special thanks to S and A, the PSNI and to the one person who has saved my life on a number of occasions, and without whom I would not be here.

Last, but not least, my family.

DOUBLE AGENT

The authors would like to salute all those individuals who risked so much and sacrificed so much to help us. Most of all, we would like to thank our families for supporting us during the researching and writing of this book.

CONTENTS

CONTENTS

FOREWORD BY MARTIN INGRAM

The world of a double agent is a dangerous one, and a complicated one. But there are basic rules. Rules that should be adhered to by agents, and by their 'handlers' – the men charged with plotting their progress. These basic rules are in place to ensure that agents and their handlers are aware of their limitations, limitations imposed by common law and decency. In the case of Kevin Fulton, these rules were flouted, again and again.

Put simply, the role of an agent is to protect life and property by gathering intelligence about a particular target – be it an individual or a grouping – in this case, the Provisional IRA. The role of the agent's handler is to maximise this gleaned intelligence, and to use it against the specific target. But the handlers in the case of Kevin Fulton broke the rules of common law and decency. And because they broke the rules, so too did Kevin Fulton.

Kevin Fulton was a British agent actively encouraged to take part in operations that were immoral, and illegal. In effect, he was handed a licence to kill by British military intelligence, through its secret wing, the Force Research Unit (FRU). When you read this book, be under no illusion that Fulton took part in operations that resulted in murders, with the full knowledge of FRU. His police handlers knew it. His military handlers knew it. The British State knew it. And, later, so did the families of his victims.

Legally, Fulton can't directly admit to his role in murdering people while employed by the State. To do this would be an invitation for the State to lock him up and throw away the key. As you will deduce from this book's devastating revelations, the State would like nothing better than to lock up Kevin Fulton, and to throw away the key.

For his part, Fulton would like nothing better than to tell the *whole* truth about the terrorism he wreaked with the full knowledge of British intelligence. He'd like nothing better than to fully expose the truth about Northern Ireland's 'Dirty War', and how agencies of the British State encouraged his illegal action. Most of all, Kevin Fulton would love to reveal the full truth as to how these agencies conspired with other agents to have him killed, once he'd served his purpose.

He can't tell the whole truth. One day he will. In the meantime, in *Unsung Hero*, Fulton goes further than any other agent in describing the horror of Britain's Dirty War in Northern Ireland.

KEVIN FULTON

And he's telling the truth. How do I know? Because I used to work for his employer, the British army's disgraced Force Research Unit

I first met Fulton at the Shelbourne Hotel in Dublin in 1999. I was asked along by Liam Clarke, the *Sunday Times* Northern Ireland editor. Clarke had asked me to meet with Fulton to see if I could help him gain compensation from the Ministry of Defence for the work he'd carried out as a double agent. I had my own motivations for meeting Fulton. I was desperate to hear more and learn more about the IRA's security department. I was able to corroborate his claims with key sources within British intelligence, within Northern Ireland security services and within the Provisional IRA.

It quickly became clear that Fulton *is* telling the truth.

Initially, I have to admit to feeling sceptical about meeting with this murderer. Even today, we continue to disagree about the politics of Northern Ireland. That said, Fulton has never lied to me. He has never exaggerated or diminished his own role in any terrorist operations. I am also happy to record that I like Kevin Fulton as an individual.

I soon realised that Fulton's singular fault lay in his conviction that, as an agent of the Crown, he *did* have a licence to kill. I try to tell him he didn't, but I've come to the conclusion that, such was Fulton's trust for his handlers, that, when they told him he had a licence to kill, he believed them. He believed them because, for 15 years, he'd put his life into their hands.

Then, when he was no longer of use to them, he was betrayed and abandoned. He remains abandoned to this day.

Why is the State so keen to abandon Fulton to the murderous whim of former members of the Provisional IRA, who Fulton helped to convict? After reading this book, you'll discover the answer. Amid the swirling murk of Northern Ireland politics, it is clear and it is depressing.

The public doesn't realise is that, without Fulton, the truth about the Omagh bombing would not be known. And countless murderous Provisional IRA operations would not have been thwarted. For these reasons, he deserves what his former employers promised, but then denied him – the security of life away from constant death threats, displacement and an inability to secure any kind of proper job.

He has been shafted by the very people for whom he risked his life, daily. Whether or not one agrees with the tactics used by his employers, Kevin Fulton deserves to be protected.

Martin Ingram, ex-officer, Force Research Unit

PREFACE

M y wife always knew me as an IRA man. Nothing else. Twenty-one years on, I finally told her the truth.

She thought I was joking.

Nobody – not my closest family, not the highest figures within the IRA – had the slightest inkling of my true identity. Twenty-one years of living a lie. During all that time, I was really working for the British intelligence services. I was a double agent within the world's most feared terrorist organisation.

I'm not a grass. I'm not someone who crossed over to the other side to save my own skin. I was a British soldier, actively recruited by British military intelligence for the specific task of infiltrating the IRA and working my way up within the organisation. Which is exactly what I did.

Such was my efficiency as an IRA man, I was eventually

promoted to the 'nutting squad' – the terrorist organisation's feared internal security unit charged with rooting out and killing informants. Some say that my promotion was testament to my steely nerve and to the skill of my handlers who delighted in the rich irony of this role; others insist that I was actively encouraged to go too far to maintain my cover as a top IRA operative. They say that, in the interests of keeping me on side with IRA chiefs, I was allowed to carry out morally reprehensible acts against my own people.

It is true that, as an agent for the British Crown, I helped shoot and kill British soldiers, police informants and members of the Royal Ulster Constabulary.

People on my own side.

I played a key role in the slaying of army comrades and decent law-abiding members of the police force. It gnaws at my nerves and haunts my every thought. After all, these were people striving for everything I believed in. A night will never pass without stabbings of guilt, without my brain being pulled under by great waves of confusion and doubt.

So why did I carry on? Because, all the while, I was being assured that my work was saving more lives than it was costing. That people's lives hinged on my soldiering on. That the British prime minister, no less, was being kept abreast of my great work. All along, I was being assured of something else, too. Over and over again, I was assured that if it all went wrong – if the IRA discovered my true role as a British agent – I'd be pulled out and given a new identity, a new home abroad and a lump sum.

Then my usefulness ran out, and I was dumped. Sacrificed.

KEVIN FULTON

After dedicating my life to British intelligence, they tried to get me whacked. When that didn't happen, I was abandoned. No new identity, no new home abroad, no lump sum. I was left to fend for myself. I now live life on the run, under a death threat from the IRA. Needless to say, I can't go back to Northern Ireland where my wife and family still live.

To this day, British intelligence agencies refuse to acknowledge the full extent of my role in the Dirty War. In truth, they'd like me dead. I'm a nuisance. Along the way, I've also earned the wrath of the RUC and leading dissident IRA terrorists.

In short, I don't expect to live long.

So why am I telling my story? They all counted on me disappearing, on running for my life. But I don't have a life. I've got nothing left to lose.

CHAPTER ONE

All I ever wanted was to be a British soldier.

As a young boy, I loved war movies and guns and tanks and soldiers. But, whereas most boys had to rely on the cinema for their military fix, I had the real thing, both at home and at the end of the street.

At home, my grandfather regaled me with tales of derring-do at Dunkirk. Steel Chest McGuinness they called him, on account of the shrapnel that stayed lodged near his heart until the day he died. Like many thousands of Northern Irish Catholics, he had fought in the British army in World War II and was proud of the fact.

He had a rapt audience of one: me.

Before the so-called Troubles, it wasn't unusual for Catholics to join the British army or the Royal Ulster

Constabulary. I had a cousin in the RUC and another in the Royal Irish Rangers, a famous British army regiment. As I would find out later in life, many senior Republicans served in the British army too. As an apprenticeship in warfare, British army training is considered second-to-none.

I was certainly impressed with the British soldiers I saw daily at the end of my street. I must have been eight or nine when they first came to my home town, Newry in County Down. It was the late sixties and, to us kids, the strutting, mean-eyed men in uniform were an exotic diversion. We were as transfixed by their sub-machine guns as they were bemused by our hero worship. Eventually they gave in and let us try on their helmets and look through the sights on their machine guns.

My love of all things military was sealed.

And then it all changed. After one particular Sunday afternoon, nothing was ever the same again, and the cocky, funny-sounding soldiers stopped being our friends. The day had got off to an odd start. I was the second youngest of six kids, and a real handful, and my parents were only too happy to see me running off out to play with my pals. But on this particular Sunday, they had plans for me. Dad insisted I come with him to help wallpaper a friend's sitting room. That was the day's first surprise.

I remember the house. It was close to the gasworks overlooking the town. We were munching on ham and tomato sandwiches when I heard the sound down below. It was like a crowd at a football match, but this was no football crowd. This noise had no swell or ebb, no bursts of joy or dismay. This was a constant marching rhythm, an angry heartbeat which thumped louder and louder as the day went on.

It must have been three hours later when, from the Derrybeg Estate, came the shouting and the charging and the screams of women; glass was smashing, and everywhere there was the eerie rumble of human chaos. And then a sound I'll never forget, a sound that stopped my dad dead in his tracks: gunshots crackled across the valley. Veils of smoke rose like ghosts from below, and my eyes started to sting. 'It's just the fumes from the wallpaper stripper,' said Dad, but I knew it was something else, something that, at a stroke, had tamed the raging streets.

All the next day, St Patrick's primary school was abuzz with tales from the civil rights march. The Derrybeg boys spoke of petrol bombs and baton charges and plastic bullets and barricades and tear gas. How I envied their luck at being there, on the frontline.

Back at home that evening, my enthusiasm for civil unrest was met with short shrift. My family is strictly non-political. Civil rights were the concern of other people. Dad's homeware business was doing nicely, and, sure, weren't some of our best clients Protestant? The Fultons saw no point in rocking the boat. Things were different for the people of Derrybeg, one of the hardest estates in Newry, a bogeyman neighbourhood where, somewhere along the line, grown-ups had somehow convinced me that bad things always happened.

Then Kevin Heatley got shot, and it all changed again.

It was a Saturday night in Derrybeg in 1973 when a

group of British soldiers went charging through the estate, blowing whistles and roaring their heads off. Locals came out to have a go, and suddenly a shot rang out. A British soldier had opened fire. Kevin had been sitting on a wall near his home when the bullet struck him in the head. He died later that night.

Kevin Heatley was thirteen years old – the same age as me.

That finished my parents off. From that night on, I laboured under an inflexible curfew of seven in the evening, school nights, weekends and holidays. It pained me: all the excitement happened at night when the streets bristled with clandestine subversion and, every now and then, all-out anarchy. While my friends relished nightly games of guerrilla warfare, I lay in my bedroom reading my *Boy's Own* magazines and military adventure books, dreaming that one day I'd be in the thick of the action. I wanted to join a British army regiment that didn't serve in Northern Ireland. In my dreams, I'd be on a frontline in some far-flung exotic place – perhaps a steaming Asian jungle – fighting on the side of good with honour and courage, far away from the mess of Northern Ireland.

Each morning on my way to town, I made the detour past the army recruitment centre on Cecil Street to stare at the model of an amphibian army truck in the window. It was a glorious creation with a huge mounted machine gun and massive tyres. To me, that model truck embodied the brutal perfection of army life, and reinforced my dream of one day wearing the uniform.

I must have been twelve when they blew it up. I was at my

auntie's when news came through on the radio. I ran all the way to Cecil Street, praying that my truck had survived. Amid the inevitable chaos, I fully intended to duck in under the incident tape and rescue it. Of course, the army recruitment centre had been flattened. Not one discernible shred of my Jeep remained. I vowed there and then that, one day, I would drive a real one. No matter what.

It was 1974, and even naïve, non-political, fourteen-year-old me realised that my ambition to join the British army would not be well received. Indeed, many in Newry would consider it outright betrayal of my Catholic roots. If people were to find out, then at best my family would be ostracised by the more Republican-leaning people of the town; at worst they would be persecuted and vilified. After all, Newry is 95 per cent Catholic. There was only one thing for it. I had to keep my plans to myself until such time that I could make a clean break from Newry. One day, I saw my chance.

In 1977, aged sixteen, I decided to join the merchant navy. OK, it wasn't the military, but it seemed the next best thing for now. It promised adventures and foreign travel, real *Boy's Own* stuff. My parents were delighted. They were desperate to get me away from Newry. After all, career prospects were non-existent. A lack of focus in life saw half the young lads I grew up with drifting into Republicanism. If you are congregating there on street corners, it's inevitable you get drawn in too. You start off ducking and diving and into petty crime, and suddenly you're in the lair of the Provisional IRA. The merchant navy would take me away from these dangers and give me the stimulation my hyperactive character so craved.

Wearing the black merchant-navy uniform, learning how to fight fires, sleeping in a dormitory, I found my twelve-week training stint at the National Sea Training Centre in Gravesend, Kent, military heaven. Gung-ho for action, I signed up for a six-month voyage on the Cunard steam ship *MV Andria*. I was sixteen and in for a shock.

I travelled to the United States, Japan, the Panama Canal and Chile, but soon one port looked the same as the next. It was boring. I didn't drink – I was still a child, after all – and was happy to miss out on the boozing, fighting and shagging that erupted whenever we docked at some unsuspecting port. In between these uneventful stops, I encountered a tedium that only the Ancient Mariner himself could have fully appreciated. For day after day after day, there was simply no action and nothing to see but sea and sea and more sea.

I disembarked after six months with £1,000 and a determination not to set foot on a ship again for quite some time. For months, I lived the life of Riley back home, inevitably squandering the money I'd amassed on the high seas. Soon I was seeking out a new career.

The only work going in Newry was in the meat factory. At some stage, everyone worked in the meat factory. It is as tedious as it is gruelling and depressing. Surrounded by death, morbid thoughts are an occupational hazard. Every minute of every day, automated rails of staring carcasses ghost by to the squelching soundtrack of butchery. It forces you to think about the fragility of life, and how easy it can be snuffed out. Mind you, there was plenty happening outside the slaughterhouse to remind you of this, too.

It was 1978 and the IRA had taken to planting bombs randomly in busy streets, slaughtering Catholic and Protestant civilians alike. Loyalist paramilitaries were busy targeting innocent Catholics going about their everyday business. As far as I could see, it was all to get at the British government. To me, only the British army stood in the way of Northern Ireland slipping into the abyss. The misery in the meat factory redoubled my determination to join the British army. After all, they were the good guys and army life seemed exciting, noble and clear-cut.

The day I travelled to Belfast to sign up, I didn't tell another soul. As far as my parents were concerned, I was heading to Belfast to check out the availability of another merchant-navy cruise. I didn't want to worry them. If I needed a reminder of the risk I was taking, it came at the Grand Central Hotel on Royal Avenue where the army was holding its recruitment day. The entire building was caged in; sandbags were piled up as high as the first floor; soldiers were swarming everywhere. While it might have rattled some, it sent a bolt of anticipation through me. Risk, power, combat – this was what I wanted.

I sat an exam. I signed forms. I was told to go home and wait for security clearance. I gave them my aunt's address for any correspondence. Days later, the security clearance arrived. I told my family I was off to London for another stint on the merchant-navy boats, and headed back to the recruitment centre in Belfast. Myself and the other eager recruits were driven by minibus to the Palace Barracks in Holywood, just outside Belfast. We ate, we met other soldiers, we swore allegiance to the Queen and we received our ceremonial Queen's shilling. And that was it. I was in the British army.

The next day, we headed to Sutton Coldfield, near Birmingham, for a three-day induction. The ferry to Liverpool was full of soldiers in full uniform. Some people dream of a certain type of home or a particular make of car. I dreamed of that uniform. Travelling with me were four other raw recruits, all Protestant and vociferously puzzled by my life choice. Their bafflement didn't offend me in the slightest. After all, I wasn't a bigot. Being brought up in Newry, I didn't know any Protestants to be bigoted against. I explained to them that this was my dream and I was going to pursue it, no matter what. Religion, I pointed out with gusto, meant *nothing* to me. Little did I know that my religion would mean *everything* to the army.

Over the next few days, news of a Catholic within the ranks had obviously spread. Repeatedly, complete strangers enquired as to whether I 'kicked with the right or left foot'. Assuming I was being sized up for some sort of soccer competition, I stated that I kicked with my right foot, though not terribly well. Such was my dread of sports that I was almost relieved to discover that it was a coded question, aimed at establishing my religious persuasion. A 'left footer' is Protestant slang for a Catholic. How was I to know?

Up until then, I had met one Protestant my own age. I had never met a black or Asian person. The remainder of those three days in Sutton Coldfield were a multi-cultural crash course in which I strove not to be caught out again. I didn't want to appear too green.

Conversely, finding myself flung into the prosaic real world made me take stock of my own identity and its inherent contradictions. I'm a British citizen but consider myself Irish. When it came to choosing a regiment, one seemed to fit the bill: the Royal Irish Rangers.

At that time, the Rangers didn't serve in the six counties. Regimental Sergeant Major Bobby Orr had impressed me when he insisted, 'We're an Irish regiment. There's no religion, we're just one big family.'

I was to discover otherwise.

Committing to the Rangers had one down side – a twelve-week training stint in Ballymena, County Antrim. Ballymena is as Protestant as Newry is Catholic, and it wasn't long before my status as a left footer was known to all and sundry. Twice I was called a 'Fenian bastard'. One senior army officer insisted on writing down my religious persuasion on a recruitment form in pencil, as he was convinced I would soon change my mind. I saw it as deliberate baiting, part of my training. I knew I wasn't going to beat them, so I decided I might as well join them. I learned the words of a few UVF songs. Whenever someone started taking the piss, I sang them loudly. It worked. They weren't going to get a rise out of me.

Besides, I was having too good a time to care. Here I was in army uniform, firing guns and hurling grenades and living the life I'd dreamed of since childhood. My rampant enthusiasm saw me volunteering for everything – I even missed leave to go on exercises. 'Army Barmy' – that's what my fellow soldiers called me, and my passion for the uniform soon seemed to eclipse the apparent handicap of being a Catholic.

By the end of those twelve weeks, I was convinced that my Catholicism was no longer an issue. Little did I know that my status as a Catholic from Newry was about to become the cornerstone of my entire military career.

It all started in June 1979. I was training with the Anzio platoon when Sergeant Joe Moore took me to one side. 'Fulton, get down to the Education Centre at once. There's someone there to see you,' he said.

Shit, I thought.

Sergeant Moore read my mind. 'You're not in any trouble, Fulton,' he said. 'These people want to know if you can help them with a small matter. That's all.'

I still didn't like it. I knocked on the door with as much confidence as I could muster. Behind a desk sat a scruffy man and behind him, clearly transfixed by something outside, stood a shorter man in casual clothes.

'Please, sit down,' said the first man in an English accent.

He introduced himself as Gerry, the other man as Andy, and that was it as far as introductions went. 'Don't worry, Kevin,' said Gerry firmly, 'we simply want you to assist us in one small matter.'

Although I had no inkling of it then, that 'small matter' set in motion a sequence of extraordinary events that would cast a long shadow over the rest of my life. Gerry and Andy, as I learned much later, were from the Force Research Unit, a secretive and controversial group within the British military.

Set up in 1980, its specific purpose was to recruit people who would spy on terrorist activities.

He produced an envelope from the inside pocket of his jacket and pulled out a photograph. 'You're from Newry, Kevin, isn't that right?' asked Gerry.

'I am indeed,' I said, still disobeying his earlier order not to worry.

He slid the photo across the desk towards me. 'Do you recognise him?' he said.

I inspected it carefully. I really wanted to say yes, but I didn't know the man from Adam. I did recognise the building behind him though. 'No,' I said, not looking up from the image, 'sorry, I don't. That's the Newry dole office behind him though,' I added, by way of compensation.

'It is indeed,' said Andy in a gruff Scots accent, still preoccupied by something out the window, 'and what better place to photograph the young male Catholic population of Newry!'

'Too true,' I said, as Gerry slid over another photo. Then another. Finally, by snap seven, I was able to recognise someone. An old school friend, an innocent enough fellow. I told them as much and they seemed terribly pleased. For my part, I felt like I'd passed some sort of test.

'We've set up a covert observation post there,' said Andy, who then turned towards me and looked into my eyes for the first time. 'Can you come back next week and look at some more photos?'

'No problem,' I said eagerly, 'only too happy to help.'

'Excellent,' said Gerry. 'You've no idea how important this

is to us, Kevin. In fact, even your sergeant isn't to know what went on here today. Understood?'

'And if anybody asks why you were called out of training,' said Andy, 'just say you had to see someone from army welfare. Personal matter.'

'No problem,' I said, though I was still puzzled. I had managed to identify an out-of-work school-leaver from Newry. Could this really be of such critical importance to the British military? I returned to routine army life somewhat perplexed. Who were these people? Who did they work for? Was it better that I hadn't asked?

It all served to make me more paranoid about being Catholic. 'You'd think we were fucking aliens!' I remember complaining to another 'left footer' in the Rangers, who hailed from Longford in the Irish Republic.

But I was eighteen and eager to impress, so a week later I trooped back dutifully to the Education Centre and thumbed through more grainy photographs of Newry's unemployed. What a sorry lot they were too – surely more a threat to good fashion sense than to national security, I thought. I coughed up what names and personal details I could, though the snippets of information I provided seemed laughably banal to me. Over and over again, I apologised for my failure to provide anything I considered of substance or significance.

'You're doing absolutely fine,' Gerry reassured me just as often. 'These are all vital pieces in the intelligence jigsaw.' At least now I knew where they were from.

Over the following weeks and months, I studied endless photographs and told Andy and Gerry everything I knew about IRA sympathisers in Newry, right down to the cars they drove and the pubs they drank in. They in turn freely regaled me with tales from Bessbrook, the British intelligence Force Research Unit's HQ in South Armagh where they were based. To an eighteen-year-old raw recruit, their stories of high-risk espionage and intrigue sounded better than James Bond. From what I could gather, these men had a licence to do whatever they wanted. I could tell they enjoyed impressing me and, when the opportunity came to show off their powers, they jumped at the chance.

I told them how my family believed I was sailing around the globe with the merchant navy, not serving with a British army regiment forty miles up the road in Antrim. Trouble was, it had been months since they'd got a postcard. I was worried they would twig.

'Leave it to us,' said Gerry and, a week later, they arrived with a postcard.

'Write your message,' said Andy, 'and we'll get it posted to them from somewhere exotic. Where d'ya fancy?'

From that point on, my family received postcards from me regularly, posted in different locations all over the world. I could scarcely believe they were going to all this trouble for me – just a number in the British army. I felt we were becoming good friends. I liked them both. However, I always left the Education Centre feeling as if I had let them down somehow. I sensed they were always a little disappointed with my information. They never said so, but I felt guilty. I mean, two hotshots from military intelligence coming to see me and all I could provide was harmless tittle-tattle.

It was Gerry who sensed my frustration. After a dozen or so meetings, one week he cut to the chase. 'Do you know other young lads who might be able to help us?' he asked. 'Anyone you could introduce us to?'

I did have a couple of close friends, but could they be trusted? Clearly, it would involve me telling them I was in the British army.

'Just let us meet some of these friends,' said Andy, 'and we'll do the rest.'

I felt I had to take the risk. That weekend, I went home to Newry. The family was thrilled to see me. I regurgitated versions of stories I had heard during my original spell with the merchant navy, and nobody seemed to suspect a thing. I went out that night and caught up with people I hadn't seen in nearly a year. Once again, my merchant-navy story went unchallenged. I found the deception effortless and, in the end, I began to enjoy it. Little did I know that my cover would be blown that night anyhow, in a way I could never have foreseen.

I got home at three in the morning to find my mother in the kitchen, hunched over. I could tell she had been crying.

'What's up, Mum?'

She unfurled her fingers, still clutching a tissue, to reveal something in the palm of her hand. It was my army identification document.

'Ach, I was gonna tell you,' I started, but the words shrivelled up. Suddenly, my mum looked old and fragile and very tired. I put my hand on her shoulder and told her not to be worrying herself about it.

14

'Don't be worrying meself?' she gasped incredulously, looking up at me sharply. 'What do you mean don't be worrying meself about it? If *they* find out *they*'ll kill you!'

'Nobody'll find out. Sure, who's gonna tell them?' I said.

'For God's sakes, Kevin,' she said, 'don't you realise? Of course they'll find out. Someone always finds out.'

Of course, I knew she was right. I had just been hiding from the fact that, in Northern Ireland, there's no hiding place. There is no job or pastime or social function safe from the creeping grapevine of hate and paranoia. Of course they would find out. And then I'd be a 'legitimate target'. At best, my family would be boycotted and abused. At worst, I'd be whacked coming out of the front door some morning.

'You've gone and signed your own death warrant,' said Mum, breaking down into great heaving sobs, the army identification document tumbling out of her hand on to the kitchen floor. I scooped it up and hurried away. I couldn't stand seeing her in such pain. In my selfish rush to fulfil a childish dream, I had deluded myself into believing I could keep my entire working life a secret from my own family and my community. What an idiot I had been: I had put my family at risk; I had destroyed my mother's peace of mind for good; I had committed her to a vocation of pain and worry. For the rest of her days, every time the phone would ring or the doorbell sound, she would be bracing herself for the news. That night was one of the lowest of my life.

I didn't sleep much. I knew that two more people were about to find out about my secret life as a soldier in the British army. I arranged to meet two close friends in a pub the next afternoon for a game of pool. Somehow, I had to persuade them to meet Andy and Gerry. In the end, I told them Andy and Gerry were friends from the merchant navy. Would they fancy going to a nice pub in the country that Wednesday to meet them? Maybe have a few jars and a bite to eat? When I told them that my new friends were loaded and offering to pay, there was no hesitation.

That night, as instructed, I rang Gerry on a special number and told him the news. I felt like I had passed my first major test. Gerry was thrilled. I'll always remember his words. 'You know, you're really cut out for this, Kevin,' he said.

The compliment failed to cheer. I felt low. The thought of my mother back home worrying about me made me feel ashamed. Sensing my subdued mood, Gerry told me I should be feeling proud of myself. 'I suppose so,' I replied cryptically.

That Wednesday, I introduced Andy and Gerry to my two friends. The night was purely social – no mention of intelligence or the military – and everyone got on famously. Soon we were a regular social group. I watched Andy and Gerry cultivate the two men as friends: within weeks, Andy was teaching one of them to drive, and Gerry was helping the other lad get a loan to buy a car. They stood us a good many pints and joked about how there was money to be earned just by helping in really simple ways.

By now, Andy and Gerry were ringing up my friends and asking them to go and check if a certain car was outside a certain house. They would ask who lived at number 42, and whether they were believed to be up to anything dodgy. They were all pieces in the intelligence jigsaw, and now they had two willing and watching sets of eyes and ears in the heart of two housing estates in Newry. Combined with all the latest local gossip, the British military had probably never before had a place so sewn up for intelligence.

Gerry and Andy were delighted, as they told me at our weekly private get-togethers in the Army Education Centre. They started asking me if I would be interested in working for military intelligence. 'You know I live for the army,' I said, suspecting that it was no more than idle flattery. However, the hollowness of the words as they came out surprised me. Now that my mother knew the truth, and was probably worrying herself sick about it, the army no longer seemed the dream life it once did.

On the other hand, the prospect of working for military intelligence scared me to death. I felt intimidated by the very notion of intelligence work. It seemed a shadowy other-world, way beyond my rudimentary political understanding. Looking back, perhaps it was my political naïvety that made me such an attractive catch to the intelligence services.

They let it be known to me that their superiors were all for giving me a job, as I was considered the perfect recruit. I simply couldn't see it. How could a squaddie with few qualifications be of such worth to British military intelligence?

'Have you heard of Captain Robert Nairac?' Gerry asked me one Wednesday.

'Of course I have,' I said. 'I used to work in the meat factory, didn't I?'

They looked at me quizzically.

Captain Robert Nairac was the senior British soldier who

tried to infiltrate the IRA. He put on a Northern Irish accent, invented an Irish background and learned the words to a few rebel songs. Needless to say, he was rumbled. Northern Ireland is like a village, and it didn't take long for IRA top brass to realise he was an impostor. A few years earlier, in May 1977, it was widely reported how Captain Nairac had disappeared. Eventually, the IRA admitted interrogating and executing him. However, they had never handed over Nairac's body. While working in the meat factory in Newry, I found out why. Some short-term contract workers in Newry had been working at the company's sister factory in Dundalk at the time of Nairac's disappearance. I told Andy and Gerry what I had heard. 'They put him through the mincer,' I said, as sensitively as one can say such a thing.

They looked stunned. Sickened.

'What?' said Gerry.

'They scalped him, cut out his innards and turned him into meat and meal.'

'But why?' said Andy. 'Why didn't they dump his body in a ditch?'

'Apparently, he'd been so badly tortured and beaten, he was unrecognisable,' I said. 'The IRA didn't want it known how badly he'd been treated. The meat factory is full of Provos, so they, er, got rid of the body.'

'God,' said Andy quietly.

It was me who broke the silence. 'So, what about Captain Nairac?' I said.

'Oh, well,' said Gerry awkwardly, 'seems almost sick to bring it up now, but he was trying to infiltrate the IRA. Of course, it was hopelessly misguided. I mean, he was English, for Chrissakes.' I could see where this was heading. 'So there's a new policy now, a far more sensible policy. We want people from Northern Ireland, Catholics, to get inside the IRA for us, to work up through the ranks, even if it takes years.'

'I see,' I said.

'You'd be perfect,' said Gerry. 'You're a Catholic from Newry. Your family is non-political. They could check you out and you'd come through, no problem.'

'Well, yes, that's probably true,' I said hesitantly.

'Think you could do it?' said Andy.

'God, I don't know,' I said, and I really didn't. All I could see were deadly risks. All I could feel were terrified thoughts. I thought it was a good time to vent them. 'Surely they'd find out I was a British soldier. They'd put two and two together and that would be the end of it.'

Of course, Andy and Gerry had it all worked out. Joining military intelligence would mean leaving the army and returning to Newry. They agreed that news of my military career would inevitably become common knowledge, but they could fix that. I would be issued with a dishonourable discharge. They would dream up a suitably convincing story as to why I had been booted out of the British army. In disgrace. That should please the locals. From then on, I'd be a double agent. Secretly, I'd still receive my army wage each week, in cash. My new task would be to work my way into the lower levels of the Provisional IRA in Newry, then slowly, slowly work my way up the ranks. It would be a real slow burner – fifteen to twenty years – all the while providing

British intelligence with vital information. The work would be exciting, important and, best of all, I'd be personally responsible for saving countless lives. I would be a hero.

'But surely,' I countered, 'as soon as an operation goes wrong because someone has talked, they'll suspect me. I'll be in the fucking mincing machine then.'

Gerry and Andy assured me that this simply would not happen. They would act as my handlers, and my security would be their uppermost priority. Under no circumstances would they risk my safety. They already had agents inside the IRA, some of whom had been there for ten or fifteen years. Andy and Gerry had ensured no harm came to them – they were simply too valuable to be compromised in any way. If it did go wrong, they could pull me out in an instant and spirit me away to a new country with a new identity, a new home and a lump sum, where I could live out the rest of my days. More than once in the recent past, they told me, they had had to do just that to save the bacon of one of their prized agents. It is, they insisted, a contingency plan that can be exercised at a moment's notice.

'Think about it,' said Gerry, but I was incapable of thinking about anything else. What they told me was impressive. They were impressive. But I couldn't help thinking about Nairac and how easily it could all go wrong. I certainly knew only too well the calibre of the people I'd be messing with. If they were somehow to uncover my true motivation, death, when it came, would probably be a relief.

They sensed my reluctance and insisted that I wouldn't have to do anything I didn't want to. Having by now served a full year in the British army, this was a level of personal freedom to which I was no longer accustomed. The fact that I wouldn't have to do anything I didn't want to was probably the single most persuasive factor of all.

The seduction carried on for many weeks. They knew about my passion for guns. One Wednesday, as a special treat, they whisked me off to a shooting range in the middle of nowhere and let me play with Kalashnikovs and Remington Wingmasters. 'Come and work with us,' said Andy, 'and you can have access to these every day. None of your standard-issue army rubbish.'

Driving past a barracks one day, they really made me think. 'Look at that soldier there,' he said, pointing at a chubby man marching across the square. 'What good is he doing his country, eh? Plodding around a parade ground in circles?'

'But I like being a British soldier,' I said.

'You'd still be a British soldier,' said Gerry, 'but you'd be a soldier on a very special mission.'

I could recognise another bonus in working for Andy and Gerry – a quick-fix solution to a problem that was really wearing me down. I'd be able to tell my mother that I'd left the British army. What a weight off her shoulders that would be.

But leaving the army was still a wrench. The camaraderie, the physical challenges in which I revelled, the danger and the promise of live combat one day – how could I turn my back on everything I'd dreamed of since childhood?

By this stage, a short-term solution to my mother's woes had arrived in the shape of a transfer. In the autumn of 1980,

I joined the first battalion of the Royal Irish Rangers in Berlin. At least no one from Newry will spot me here, I remember thinking. But the seeds of my dissatisfaction with army life had been sown by Andy and Gerry; they blossomed in the sub-zero winter temperatures of Berlin. I was bored and cold and lonely. When an FRU officer began making overtures to me about returning to Northern Ireland to work for military intelligence, he didn't have to work too hard. It was the solution to all my woes – the cold, the loneliness, the threats to my family's safety and the overbearing boredom. I would be back with my family. My neighbours would think I had been booted out of the British army and, as such, I would be welcomed back into the bosom of latent Republican life in Newry. Best of all, I would have an exciting and important new role about which only a select few would know.

To be fair to the liaison officer, he did warn me of the down sides. 'There's no medals for this work, Fulton,' he said grimly one night, 'no official recognition. If you're found dead in a ditch, we won't claim you. We won't be telling them that we managed to get someone inside their organisation. You'll die an IRA terrorist.'

The irony of this new reality really stung me. All I ever wanted was to be a British soldier.

CHAPTER TWO

On 26 May 1981, I was demobbed from the British army. It was three weeks to the day since IRA prisoner Bobby Sands died in the H-block of Long Kesh Prison after sixty-six days on hunger strike. I returned to a very different Newry, a very different Northern Ireland. The death of Bobby Sands pulled the pin out of the grenade.

I had been away with the merchant navy when it all started in the spring of 1978, three years earlier. Republican prisoners had been stripped of their special-category status as political prisoners and ordered to wear regulation prison clothing. They refused, claiming it categorised them as 'ordinary criminals'. In protest at the loss of special-category status, which they had retained since 1972, they took to wearing only blankets in their cells – this group became known as the blanket men. They soon escalated their campaign by refusing to wash or to use the toilets; they smashed up the furniture in their cells and smeared the walls with their own excrement. The Dirty Protest had begun. By the time I returned in May 1981, Bobby Sands and two more so-called blanket men had starved themselves to death. Their sacrifice had inspired a vast wave of support throughout the nationalist community in Northern Ireland, particularly in Catholic towns like Newry.

I returned to Newry the day they buried the third dead hunger striker. Raymond McCreesh was from Camlough in South Armagh, just a few miles from Newry, and had been educated at St Colman's, a Catholic secondary school in the town. The black flags draped from every building summed up the mood of the town.

All of Northern Ireland's repressed nationalist rage seemed bottled up in Newry that afternoon. It felt as if the town itself was ticking, like a primed bomb. I felt nervous. Conspicuous. If word spread amongst these mourners that I was a British agent, I would have been lynched there and then. To these people, my people, I was the enemy. It would have done me no good whatsoever explaining to these wounded Catholic souls that I actually had some sympathy for the hunger strikers. Before then, I'd always considered IRA members to be mere gut Republicans, an Armalite in one hand and a set of rosary beads in the other. But the men of the H-block seemed different, idealistic. However, these sympathies were tempered by the knowledge that days earlier, on 19 May 1981, five of my British army comrades had been blown up by an IRA landmine just a few miles from Newry – five working-class boys just like Bobby Sands and Raymond

McCreesh, except that these five dead soldiers hadn't been politically motivated, and they hadn't chosen to die.

And so I didn't skulk past these mourners with my head down. Instead, I took a deep breath and vowed to myself that I would avenge the deaths of my five army comrades by infiltrating the very organisation that had murdered them. For the first time since I had agreed to work as a double agent, I felt not just excitement and terror. I felt confidence. For a start, I was returning to my home town of Newry and to people I knew and understood. Bizarrely, I had more in common with the local corner boys who were desperate to become IRA volunteers than with my fellow British soldiers. I knew I would have no problems presenting myself to senior IRA figures as yet another disenfranchised raw recruit. I suppose that's why I had been hand picked for the job.

And that was the second major spur for me. Here I was, a lowly teenage squaddie with no formal qualifications, being groomed for a role as a special agent, chosen by military intelligence to become their man in Newry, and getting paid my army wage to live out this *Boy's Own* adventure! That I had been singled out by Andy and Gerry – two men of unquestioned calibre and standing – made me feel ten feet tall. I was bowled over.

So, while Newry marched sombrely behind Raymond McCreesh's coffin, I embarked on my new life. Special Agent Fulton met Andy and Gerry every Wednesday afternoon. Even these meetings were the stuff of spy movies. We always met at a lay-by or in a car park. I would drive past first to check no other vehicle was loitering. If it was all clear, I would pull in and call my special number from the phone box. Within minutes, an unmarked saloon car with tinted windows would pull in. An unnamed intelligence officer would jump out, hop into my car and drive off, and I would join Andy and Gerry.

I was driving to yet another clandestine meeting one Wednesday when I suddenly noticed something sinister. At a junction, a man sat in a stationary car watching me intently as I drove past. At the next junction sat another motionless car containing another solitary figure seemingly intrigued by my passing. At the next junction, another. Then another. Struck by paranoid terror, I skidded to a halt, wheeled round and headed straight back home. Sick with panic, I ran in and dialled the number to my handlers. I'd been rumbled already. They had to get me out.

Gerry laughed for what seemed like several minutes. He finally recovered enough to tell me that the men in parked cars were on our side. They were intelligence agents. They had been there every Wednesday, observing my passage to our secret meetings, ensuring I wasn't being tailed. It had taken me several weeks to spot them. I felt myself blushing, not out of embarrassment but out of pride. In all my life, I had never felt so important. All this effort every single Wednesday, just to preserve my safety!

Typically, once we had safely negotiated the rendezvous, the three of us would head off for the afternoon. I never knew where we were going or what was planned, but I was never disappointed. In five-star hotel rooms, they taught me the black arts of counter-surveillance, covert photography and lock-picking while I helped myself to room service. I was presented

26

with an expensive camera and a state-of-the-art development kit, which they instructed me to keep in the basement room of a cousin's house. I was given a set of skeleton keys and taught how to open any standard five-pin tumbler lock or padlock. All this I grasped quickly and easily. I believed myself a natural. I wanted to get out there straight away and start snapping terrorist suspects and breaking into their illicit weapons dumps. But each week, I was told I wasn't quite ready yet. After about three months, I was growing impatient.

'What are you talking about?' I demanded to know one particular week. 'I've mastered all the skills! What's there to wait for?'

'You can't just go rushing in there, Kevin,' Andy said. 'They'll smell a rat and you'll be down a hole.'

Looking back, I wasn't remotely ready for the challenge ahead. The gung-ho bravura of army life had no place in this new vocation of watching and waiting. I was still a soldier, as Gerry summed up one week in his own inimitable way.

'For Christ's sake, Kevin,' he barked, 'take the poker out of your hole. You look like your spine's going to snap. Anyone can see you're a soldier a mile off.'

Getting me mentally right was the real challenge for my handlers. All I ever wanted was to be a British soldier. Now suddenly I realised that, to succeed in my new mission, I would have to *become* an IRA man. I'd have to live the lie twenty-four hours a day, seven days a week. To the police, to my friends, to my own family, I would be an IRA man.

Yet, by the same token, Andy and Gerry were insistent that I make no secret of my stint in the British army. I wanted to stick with my merchant-navy tale, but they figured that even the most rudimentary check would uncover my secret and I would be summarily executed. They decided instead to change the nature of my short but impeccable military career.

I had received an exemplary discharge book from the British army, which I still cherish to this day. However, after my handlers pulled some strings, I was issued with a second discharge book from the Royal Irish Rangers. This alternative discharge book outlined how I was unsuited to army life, and how I had left under a cloud after disobeying orders. If further clarification was sought by anyone, I had my story ready. I had been caught drinking in a particular bar in Berlin. Back then, this bar was a notorious Republican pub that collected for the INLA and was strictly out of bounds for squaddies. If you got caught drinking there, you were out. Simple as that. At a stroke, my life story had been rewritten. Once again, it seemed to me that my handlers could fix just about anything. These boys could perform miracles.

On one occasion, my CB radio was impounded at the border. I told my handlers and, next morning at nine o'clock, they delivered it back to me personally. On another occasion, Andy and Gerry asked me to check out the contents of a lock-up garage on the outskirts of Newry. They gave me an exact time to break in and, sure enough, at that exact moment, as if by magic, the streets emptied of soldiers and RUC officers, a set of roadworks appeared and all passing traffic was diverted well away from my handiwork. I was seriously impressed. So, when Andy and Gerry said that if it all went wrong they could pull me out of Northern Ireland in an instant, I believed them.

I set about rehabilitating myself among the Republicans of Newry with that rescue package uppermost in my mind. Step one was to start hanging around a certain Republican drinking hole. Back then, this place in Newry was the focal point of all Republican activity. If there was a Republican march, participants would be invited to muster there. Known sympathisers and activists circulated here. It was a lavishly appointed three-storey building with a bar on two floors. The action was all up top in the snooker hall, which saw little snooker but a lot of card-playing, posturing and gossiping.

One of the regulars there was a staunch Republican and an old family friend who would later become a Sinn Fein councillor. An introduction from him was an 'open sesame' to this inner sanctum of Newry life. The premise was simple: if you start hanging about with these people, you start to blend in and become one of them; hang about with bad boys and you become a bad boy. I started hanging round the bar every night.

From the outset, I was really open about being kicked out of the army. I let it be known that I had only joined up in the first place to gain experience of guns and explosives, which I loved. Nobody seemed remotely bothered by this admission. If anything, I was disappointed by the lack of response. I was expecting to be challenged about my British army past, and so presented with the perfect chance to lay my IRA credentials on the table, as it were, to explain how I'd seen the error of my ways and now loathed all agencies of British imperialist might. But it never came to this. I was readily accepted as another disaffected local Catholic youth with typical Republican leanings. As such, it was only a matter of time before I was urged to come along to what constituted fun for the likes of us – Irish nights in the local town hall.

Run by Sinn Fein, these Irish nights were orgies of Republican rabble-rousing. Revellers showed off their impeccable Republican credentials by collecting money for IRA prisoners, belting out rebel songs at full pelt and shamelessly schmoozing the guest – usually some forlorn, bearded former prisoner from Belfast. It was at one of these Irish nights that I first clapped eyes on Eamon Collins.

I vaguely knew Eamon as an employee of Her Majesty's Customs and Excise in Newry. Tubby and balding, he was every inch the civil servant. Imagine my surprise one particular night when he stormed up on to the stage triumphantly to announce the murder of an RUC man in South Armagh. Cue the deafening roar of approval, and demonic little Eamon punching the air and milking the applause. Newry? More like Nuremberg, I thought. With that, Eamon ran back out of the town hall again.

'Holy fuck,' I said to one of the drinkers, 'doesn't he work for Customs?'

'Oh yeah,' he said, 'but he's one of the top IRA men in Newry.'

'I'd like to meet him,' I said, feigning a sort of star-struck awe.

'Ach, Eamon's not the sociable sort,' he replied. 'To be honest, the bigwigs in Belfast think he's a pain in the arse. If you left Eamon in a room on his own, he'd fall out with himself.'

Fuck, I thought, how do I get an introduction to one of these movers and shakers? I persevered with the Irish nights, convincing myself that somehow amid the drunken revelry I would locate the inner sanctum of the IRA in Newry. They were manic occasions, a bit like the Mafia gatherings I had seen in the movies. The gossip was rife – who was shagging who on the estates, whose kids were taking drugs, who had disappeared without trace, probably into the RUC's new 'supergrass' scheme. Discretion was not on the agenda.

However, as I soon discovered, genuine, hardcore IRA operatives would be careful to *avoid* events like the Irish nights, just as they would avoid high-profile IRA funerals or marches – anywhere where they could be covertly photographed or videoed by the security forces. Apparently, Eamon Collins was something of a maverick who had gone beyond caring, but any other genuine IRA activists went to great lengths to remain unknown to the police or to intelligence forces. The people attending these Irish nights were weekend rebels.

And so the real thing proved elusive. I eventually discovered I had been searching in the wrong place. It was towards the end of 1982 when the loose-tongued loafers at the club put me in the picture. By now, the hunger strikes were over. Ten prisoners were dead and the popularity of the IRA was at an all-time high. Surely this was the optimum time for the Newry branch to induct eager new recruits. But, at this critical juncture in Republican history, the IRA in Newry was in total disarray.

A highly effective four-man unit, which had wiped out my five army colleagues just outside Newry in May 1981, had disbanded en masse shortly afterwards as a result of an ongoing dispute with the leadership in Belfast. In the wake of the hunger strikes, the leadership was desperate to cash in on a fresh surge of sympathy for the IRA. A decision was made to dispatch operatives from Belfast to places like Newry to team up with the local units.

The trouble was, most of these refugees from Belfast were 'red lights'. That was the nickname given to IRA men who were known to the Crown forces – their presence in an area acted like a red light to police and the British army. Many had previous convictions for terrorism, and some were even escapees from the Maze Prison! Needless to say, local operatives who had gone to extraordinary lengths to remain unknown to the security forces did not want to operate alongside red lights from Belfast. Their cover would be blown in days. The Newry unit opted to dissolve rather than to subscribe to this ludicrous new directive. And so, despite the fact that the IRA was enjoying a surge in support, Newry had no active unit.

Meanwhile, more Belfast red lights had decamped to Dundalk across the border in the Irish Republic, and so were safely beyond the long arm of British justice. With no unit in Newry, the fugitives in Dundalk were launching attacks in Newry and County Down and then scurrying back across the border to safety.

Clearly, Dundalk was where I needed to start circulating.

With a long tradition of playing reluctant host to fugitives from Northern Ireland, Dundalk is known as El Paso. As I was about to discover, comparisons with the lawless Mexican border town were alarmingly close to the mark. All IRA men 'on the trot' headed to Dundalk. They were easy to find, whiling away their days and nights in local bars, getting pissed, picking fights with locals and stealing other IRA men's women. They acted more like an occupying force than a band of men on the run. If only those sold on the Republican ideals of Bobby Sands and the blanket men could see the flip side of the cause as presented by these ne'er-do-wells in the bars of Dundalk.

I started making the seventeen-mile journey from Newry to Dundalk every evening, and hanging about in Republican bars like the Hogan Stand, the Dundalk Bar and Aidan's Bar, and around the office of Erin Nua in Clanbrassil Street.

Erin Nua literally translates as New Ireland, and was a Sinn Fein initiative to find work for former IRA prisoners. If you wanted a plumber or someone to fix your TV, Erin Nua would supply a former IRA prisoner to do the work for you at the going rate. In effect, it was a sort of *Yellow Pages* that allowed the more radical sections of suburbia to support the cause while gaining a vital service into the bargain. God only knows what happened when you complained about the standard of work.

Yet again, mine was that strangely ubiquitous friendly face. I helped Erin Nua with a fund-raising raffle. I got to know the faces around the bars well enough to chat about football, the weather or the major news story of the moment. If I hadn't been to one of the bars for a week or two, I'd get a gentle 'ach, where've you been?' Of course, behind my back they would be making phone calls, finding out exactly who I was and whether my story stood up to scrutiny.

I told anyone who asked the same story. I joined the British army because I loved guns. I used the army to gain experience in weapons and explosives. I got kicked out after disobeying orders and drinking in a Republican bar in Berlin. I made a big deal about wanting to get out of the army anyhow as I was sick of being shat upon for being a Catholic. This still rankled with me and I held nothing but ill will for the British military. I let it be known I was a 'lilywhite' – I had no previous convictions and my family had no links to terrorists. Short of wearing a sandwich board saying 'Perfect IRA Material', I couldn't have made it clearer that I was ripe for recruitment. I honestly expected to be asked to join at any time. I just had to bide my time. If only it had been that easy.

Throughout 1983, I sipped on pints of Guinness in the lounge bars of Dundalk, a defiantly sober set of eyes and ears, looking and listening for titbits, which I would gleefully relay to Andy and Gerry. Again, it was mostly scandal about fallings out and illicit affairs – entertaining but hardly essential intelligence. Constantly they reminded me of my real mission: 'You must become one of them.'

The trouble was, after a year of trying, I felt no closer to my goal. I didn't quite know how to go about it, and nor did my handlers. I sensed they were growing as frustrated as I was. I felt guilty taking £130 a week for supplying titbits. Clearly, I couldn't walk up to known IRA men and announce that I wanted to join. They would smell a rat for sure. There was only one thing for it. I needed to show the IRA I was made of the right stuff. I needed credibility. I needed to initiate myself into the organisation.

Other young lads keen to be recruited were out stoning British soldiers or hijacking vehicles and setting them alight. With my army experience, clearly this was not an option. If I got arrested hurling petrol bombs at British soldiers, my real story would surely leak out and I would be in grave danger. I decided I needed to carry out a 'spectacular' all on my own. I thought some sort of post-office robbery would do the trick. I asked Andy and Gerry to get me a gun. They refused point blank and told me to rule out doing anything illegal unless I got their permission first. They could sense I was itching for action. A week later, they helped me launch my first offensive against the British State.

As usual, we met at our lay-by. Andy announced straight away that they had arrived at a plan. They drove me to the back end of Barcroft Park in Newry where the Dublin to Belfast rail line passes. Out we jumped, Gerry handing me a pair of gloves. 'Put them on and open the boot,' he said. Inside was a gallon can of Castrol GTX oil with a Tupperware box strapped to it. I picked it up, looked at my handlers in baffled amusement and followed them to a low wall at the edge of Barcroft Park. Over we climbed on to the railway tracks.

'Sit that there on the line,' said Andy, 'and leave the rest to us.'

A bomb-disposal team carried out a controlled explosion on my package. The rail line was shut for a week.

I rang Andy after a few days, a bit worried. The IRA would be wondering who the fuck had carried this out. 'They might be pissed off that some young lad did something without their prior consent,' I said. 'What if I'm pulled?'

'Don't be ridiculous,' said Andy. 'How could they be pissed off at a young lad attacking the British State?'

That put my mind at ease. That night at the bar, I told someone that I was the person who had put the bomb on the rail line. We'd a good laugh and soon everyone seemed to know. People I barely knew were coming up to me, saying, 'Fair fucks to ya!' Surely this showed I was made of the right stuff. Any day now, an invitation to volunteer would be forthcoming.

It never came.

My handlers decided it was best if I stuck to getting in with the big shots in Dundalk, men whose names were only whispered in Newry, such as a man who, for legal reasons, I must refer to simply as Niall.

Niall had been on the trot since January 1983 after a gunfight with the RUC on the streets of Rostrevor in County Down. Niall won; two RUC men lost their lives. This double murder cemented Niall's reputation as one of the most ruthless and effective IRA volunteers of the era, and there was no shortage of competition. Niall was still in his twenties. When I was introduced to him one night in the Dundalk Bar, he looked twice that age. I felt decidedly underwhelmed by this man – at least until he opened his mouth.

'When I heard you'd been in the army,' he said in his soft, Newry accent, 'I was going to pull you.'

I tried to suppress the terror rising inside me by laughing heartily. In that blood-curdling, freeze-framed instant, I realised I was the only one laughing. Niall was not amused. 'I only went into it because I love guns,' I said firmly. 'And then they kicked me out.'

'Is that right?' said Niall, making like he wouldn't have checked this out well before deigning to meet me.

'Oh yeah,' I said, 'dishonourable discharge. I was caught drinking in a Republican bar.'

KEVIN FULTON

'So you like guns?' said Niall, looking straight into my eyes and waiting for me to flinch.

I didn't.

'I love them, yeah,' I said.

'Me too,' he said, a glint in his eye and a smirk on his face. This time we all laughed.

Niall must have decided he was on a roll. 'I hear you've a great interest in trains too?' he said, and we all laughed hard at this one.

That was it. Andy and Gerry were thrilled. 'You've effected an introduction to one of the major players,' said Andy. 'This is a real breakthrough.'

So now I could say hello to Niall in passing. Big deal, I remember thinking. He had been hostile and intimidating – I was hardly in a position to ask him if I could join his gang. 'Keep plugging away,' my handlers kept saying. 'Slow burn. Eventually you'll get in there. You'll be one of them.'

I wanted to short-circuit all this bullshit and get straight in. I mean, what was there to wait for? How did other people get in there? Surely they had to take a chance and tell someone they wanted in. Waiting around for an invite would take forever. I decided it was time to volunteer. One night, finally, my big chance came.

I had heard the name mentioned, but I had never seen him around. To me, the man who was the IRA's officer commanding in Dundalk had attained bogeyman status. This was the boss, the man with the clout to get me in. This was the man I had to meet. But how? I had no idea what he looked like, and it wasn't the kind of question you asked around the

37

bars of Dundalk. Then, one night, I was sitting at the bar of the Hogan Stand when a thick-set, black-haired man perched himself on a stool right beside me. The first thing I noticed was his Long Kesh belt – the distinctive buckle belts made by inmates of the notorious prison and worn with such pride around Dundalk. It was then that I noticed the engraving on the buckle. It was a nickname – a nickname that only one man had in Dundalk. I realised that this was the man I was looking for. This man must be the Provisional IRA's Officer Commanding, Dundalk.

Fuck me, it's him, I almost said out loud. I couldn't believe that I would find a man with so many enemies and so much to hide swanning around like this. I didn't know whether to laugh or to run for my life.

'How are ya?' I said, to no response. Above us on a TV, a world-weary RTE reporter doled out details of a failed IRA mortar attack on an RUC station.

Fuck it, I thought to myself, this is fate giving me a nudge. I've got to go for it.

As casually but as clearly as I could, I said, 'I tell you what, myself and a friend of mine wouldn't mind joining the Provies.'

I stared intently into the head of my beer. Silence. My cheeks felt hot. Thoughts rained through my mind like sparks. Would he laugh out loud? Would he call his friends over so they could have a good laugh as well? Maybe he'll take offence and have me beaten up? They could drag me outside and give me a hiding right now. Who would argue? Maybe he'll say nothing and just walk away, leaving me to dwell on it all night? Maybe he'll mete out his punishment for this show of insolence some other time, when I'm not expecting it?

I noticed he wasn't offering to pay for his round of drinks. And the barman wasn't asking. Effortlessly, he picked up five freshly filled glasses between two comically large hands. 'Why don't you and your friend come to the Erin Nua office tomorrow night?' he said. 'Ask for me.'

'I certainly will,' I babbled. 'Thank you very much.'

'Say about half-seven,' he said, before turning and strolling back to his corner.

It was all I could do not to shout and punch the air. For three years now, I'd been trying to break into this most furtive of inner circles and I hadn't got as far as the gatekeeper. Now I was on the threshold with the local top man ready to vouch for me. By tomorrow night, I'd have the inside track. Andy and Gerry would be absolutely thrilled. All their faith in me would be repaid – with interest. Kevin Fulton, secret agent, had made his first breakthrough.

So, who was this friend? Adam, a local lad who felt bored by the prospects Newry had to offer, had said to me in passing that he'd love to join the IRA. I couldn't wait to tell him about our personal invitation, and popped in to see him on my way home that night. We both pondered whether this was all too easy. Then we thought, Well how else are you supposed to volunteer, except by volunteering? Surely now initiation into the IRA was a foregone conclusion.

The following evening, Adam and myself steeled ourselves with a quick whiskey. The short walk to the Erin Nua office seemed to take on an epic significance. I announced that we were expected to a bored face slumped at the reception desk.

'Yeah,' he said, 'follow me,' and we plodded behind him up some stairs.

I kept soothing myself with one rhetorical question: 'What's the worst that can happen?'

'Wait in there,' said the bored young man, pointing to a room on the right.

We walked in. The room had no windows. This didn't bode well. My heart was flailing like a threshing machine. My palms were slick wet, my throat powder dry. I wanted this over with. We hovered about wordlessly in the doom.

A sudden bang and I jumped a foot in the air.

'Get down on the ground. Down on the ground!'

I turned to see a man in a balaclava waving a pistol an inch from my chin.

'Get fucking down!' he shouted, grabbing my shoulder with his free hand. I hit the deck.

'What the fuck is going on?' I heard myself shout. I hadn't had time to get scared. Besides, maybe this was a test. The British army loved tests. 'Who the fuck do you think you are?' I shouted, ready to give this fucker a piece of my mind.

Next thing more feet thundered in, screaming demonically. 'Keep your fucking head down!' and a hand rammed my face into the carpet. 'Youse are fucking Brits,' said another voice, and next thing there were hands all over me. My shoes were yanked off. Then my socks. Tape around my eyes, and now I was scared. I could hear Adam being dragged off. He was moaning with fear. I thought, I'm fucked if I'm going to moan.

The belt of my trousers was undone and down came the

trousers. I was starting to think the worst now. Why the fuck are they taking off my trousers? My shirt was ripped off and my hands taped together behind my back. I was rolled over on my back and a voice, all calm, said, 'You're a British soldier, and now you want to join the IRA? Is that the story?'

It was the man I had tracked down in the bar.

'Yeah, that's the fucking story,' I shouted.

'Who knows you're here?'

'No one.'

'There's a Garda strolling about outside. A Garda we know. You brought him here, didn't you?'

'Nobody knows I'm here, I haven't told anybody.'

'So why is there a Garda outside?'

'How the fuck should I know? Look, I came here so I could fucking work for you.'

'Um, that's the story, but I don't believe a word. You're both working for the Brits.'

'I'm not. We're not. Everyone knows I was kicked out of the army.'

'Oh right,' he said. 'Well, we're taking you to Crossmaglen right now. We've taken one of your former comrades hostage. A good-looking young fella he is too, eighteen years old. I want you to put a bullet in his head. OK?'

'Fine,' I spat, anger still carrying me along. 'Take me there now and I'll fucking do it.' I suddenly noticed hands feeling my leg. 'Get your fucking hands off me,' I roared.

'So why did you join the British army then?' our interrogator asked, still spookily calm and in control, as if this scenario had been played out before him a hundred times.

'I love guns,' I panted, 'guns and bombs and stuff like that. How else was I going to get my hands on some?'

'I think you're still working for them.'

'No I am not,' I said, calm now. If there was one thing army life taught me, it was never to show fear or panic. And, if this was a test, I was determined to pass it.

Silence. Seconds heaved by. Some sort of decisive moment was arriving.

He cleared his throat. 'I'm the senior officer in this area, and I hereby order your execution,' he said.

I freaked out. A surge of panic took hold of me. They'd done their homework. They'd found out. They had moles everywhere. This was it. 'I want a proper hearing,' I shouted. 'I'm entitled to a proper hearing.'

Suddenly, hands hauled me up off the floor and I was bouncing down the stairs. All the time, hands were pawing me all over, especially my leg. I fought the hands for all I was worth, screaming so that my throat burned.

'Where's my proper hearing? You can't just do this. You can't kangaroo me. I demand a proper hearing. You fucking cunts …'

Then fresh air hit me, cold, dirty concrete beneath my bare feet. A van engine rattled near by, wafting diesel fumes across the cool night air. Christ, I thought, where are they taking me? Maybe they weren't joking about that soldier in Crossmaglen. What the fuck will I do if they ask me to shoot a British soldier?

Next to me, I heard whimpering. It was Adam. I felt another surge of indignation. I felt the courage that only those who have nothing left to lose can feel. 'Stay fucking strong, Adam,' I shouted. 'Don't give the fuckers the satisfaction.'

'Get down on your knees,' a voice shouted, blows raining in on the backs of my knees, 'say an act of contrition.'

'Which road do you want to close?' said another voice.

'What are you talking about?'

'Where do you want us to dump your body?'

'Ah, fuck off,' I said, anger sustaining me, not letting in the fear.

Fuck, this is it, I thought. I can't fucking believe it. I whispered an act of contrition and I really meant it. I was halfway through a Hail Mary when this huge bang sounded. I must have jumped a foot in the air again.

'You're next,' a voice spat in my ear, but I knew what I had heard wasn't a gunshot. It was more like someone hitting a barrel with a lump of steel. I stopped bracing myself and let my anger boil over.

'Who the fuck do you think you're dealing with?' I shouted. 'Think I'm scared of this? Go fuck yourselves. I'll be having words with some people. You won't get away with doing this to me!'

Next thing I was being manhandled again. Back up the stairs we shuffled, that hand still feeling my legs. 'Fuck off, you fucking bent bastard,' I yelled in that general direction.

I was dumped on the floor like a refuse sack. The adhesive tape was ripped from my eyes. I saw Adam on the floor next to me. All around us, five hooded men started laughing. In the middle of them, unhooded and looking like he had just been told a good one, smiled the man from the bar. I smelled piss and saw poor old Adam's wet leg. So

43

that's why they kept feeling my leg – to see if I had pissed myself too. I wasn't feeling in the least bit amused.

'Very fucking funny,' I said. 'I'll be talking to people about this.'

That seemed to make them laugh harder.

Suddenly, two mugs of tea appeared.

'Look, we have to do this. If you're still interested, come up and see me in a couple of weeks.'

Off they went, laughing and chatting as if they'd just left a good restaurant. Myself and Adam dressed in total silence, our backs to each other, shared shame surrounding us in a deafening silence.

I left Erin Nua first, got into my car and roared off, vowing never again to set foot in Dundalk.

I stopped at a phone box near Newry and rang my handlers.

'That's fucking brilliant,' said Andy on hearing of my humiliation. 'You're in. Just wait a few weeks and go back.'

'No way, José,' I said. 'There's no way I'm going back there. No way on this earth.'

'What are you talking about, Kevin?' asked Andy. 'You've cracked it. You're in.'

'Listen, I thought my number was up, Andy,' I said angrily. 'I'm not going back. I'm giving this whole thing up.'

'You've got this far, Kevin. You can't just give up now.'

'I thought I was going to be killed!'

'They were just testing you. You passed. This is what we've been working to for three years.'

'Go fuck yourselves,' I shouted, and hung up.

Right, I thought. Time to get a proper job.

CHAPTER THREE

In 1984, at the age of twenty-two, I was back in the meat factory for my second stint of misery. It was a job and I needed the money, especially now that I had new commitments.

I married my wife in March of that year. She's a Newry girl – her older brother used to hang about with my older brother – and we're still together now. Looking back, we had both lived sheltered lives. The little semi-detached home we bought on the Armagh Road represented the summit of our ambitions. If only our lives had remained that humdrum.

I fed my wife the same stories that I did my own parents and siblings and friends. As far as she was concerned, I had been booted out of the British army and now I ran around Newry with people known to be associated with the IRA. I was living a lie with my new wife, but I felt no shame. In fact, I prided myself on not telling her the truth. By doing so, I was protecting her. As long as she didn't know the truth about my work as a double agent, she couldn't be interrogated about it if my cover was blown. She didn't know anything, so she couldn't tell anybody anything and they would have to leave her alone. Letting her in on my secret life would simply put her in grave danger. She suspected nothing. Why should she?

Despite my humiliation in Dundalk, I still felt part of the IRA circle in Newry. I continued frequenting the usual bar and the Irish nights, and hanging about with known IRA sympathisers. Local RUC officers considered me 'IRA scum'. They reminded me of this fact every time I was subjected to one of their stop and searches, which happened two to three times a week, every week.

Of course, I continued meeting Andy and Gerry on Wednesdays, where I would relay the latest gossip. They continued paying me my weekly army wage, but something had changed irrevocably. On one key matter, we were deadlocked.

I refused to go back to Dundalk. Andy and Gerry couldn't hide their frustration. As far as they were concerned, I had done the hard work. Clearly, the merry hooded men had no proof that I was a double agent working for British intelligence. If they had, I would be dead. They were testing me, and I had passed that test. All I had to do was go back to see him and I would be in.

Their assessment was probably correct, but it didn't account for the fact that I was too scared to go back to Dundalk. Nor did it account for the fact that, privately, I was starting to doubt whether I was cut out for this work. The Dundalk incident seemed to me an apocryphal vision of what would happen if my cover as a secret agent was ever blown. All it would take would be one small mistake, one quirk of outrageous bad luck, and I would be on my knees in some grimy yard, saying an act of contrition and choosing which road to close. It was all very well Andy and Gerry telling me they could protect me, but what Dundalk had taught me was that, if I did infiltrate the IRA, I would be very much on my own. I would have to survive largely on my own wits, a far cry from the military life I was used to where I simply followed orders, where I enjoyed the security of being one of a vast number, where even war was a simple premise – us against them. This new life would be far more solitary, far more complicated. It would be so much harder to see the angles, to see what was going on.

The Dundalk incident made me feel vulnerable. In this nether world of intrigue and shadow, was I hopelessly out of my depth? If so, surely it was only a matter of time before I was found out by the IRA, probably tortured for information for a few days, then executed. The words of my military intelligence mentor in Berlin haunted my new recurring nightmare: 'If you're found dead in a ditch, we won't claim you. There are no medals for this work. You'll die an IRA man.'

I was twenty-two years old and recently married. I didn't fancy dying just yet. Gerry and Andy must have sensed my fragile state at this time, for they accepted my decision not to go back with good grace. 'We'd never make you do anything you didn't want to,' they always said.

So I stuck with Newry. I felt safe there. It was my home town. I knew the people and they knew me. I could see the angles. Perhaps another chance to get inside the Provisional IRA would present itself in Newry. No matter, I wasn't going back to Dundalk.

And so I carried on feeding tittle-tattle to Andy and Gerry, and picking up my weekly wage. Soon I started once more to feel guilty about taking the money. Clearly, my handlers weren't getting value for money. As the end of 1984 approached, guilt and worry gnawed away at me about our arrangement. I felt worried because I was convinced I would be dropped any day by military intelligence. If so, what would I do? Going back into the British army would mean leaving Northern Ireland, and my wife did not want to do that. The slaughterhouse represented my solitary employment prospects in Newry. Besides, I felt guilty because I was a British soldier and I was letting my side down. I had a glorious chance of getting into the IRA in Dundalk, but cowardice had got the better of me. Four years on, I was no closer to achieving the very thing I'd been recruited to do – to join the Provisional IRA.

My attempt to join had resulted in ridicule and humiliation. So I decided I needed to do something to gain credibility amongst senior IRA figures, to show how useful I could be to them. Something to show my bottle, my nerve, my enterprise. I needed to show the IRA that I had balls. I needed to approach them with some sort of a moneymaking plan.

The idea literally knocked on my door.

To supplement my unofficial army wage packet, our home

offered bed and breakfast accommodation. One of the regular visitors was a girl who I'll call Claire who was a real livewire. It didn't take her long to twig that I was ducking and diving with some of Newry's shadier characters rather than earning an honest living. Claire had an idea.

Her boyfriend, who I'll call Michael, was a lorry driver. He regularly drove lucrative loads of electrical goods to Northern Ireland from the continent. In February 1985, he was due to disembark from a ferry in Belfast with a lorry load of Mitsubishi Blue Diamond TVs and video cassette players worth about £100,000. Claire wanted to know if I would be interested in arranging for his lorry to be hijacked, in return for a cut of the profit.

I told her I'd think about it.

'This could really put you on the map,' said Gerry.

'It's perfect,' said Andy.

It did seem perfect. So perfect that I dragged two of my brothers in on the plan. However, I needed heavyweight assistance to carry off such a heist. I needed someone who could drive a large lorry and trailer. I needed somewhere to store such a voluminous bounty. Michael and Claire wanted five grand. I needed someone who could cough up five grand in cash.

Where else would I go but to the Provisional IRA?

I told my Republican contact at the IRA hangout bar about the plan. He duly reported it to his contacts within the IRA. A few days later, they generously proposed an 80/20 split – in their favour. They would supply a qualified lorry driver and somewhere to store the booty. All we had to do was a) get the lorry to stop, b) take the driver away so that their man could get into the cab and drive the load to the secret location, and c) keep our mouths shut. What could possibly go wrong?

That crisp February morning, the lorry pulled up as planned on Corporation Road, on the way out of Belfast docks. Michael hopped out, to be replaced in the cab by Dermot, a professional lorry driver and criminal from Dundalk. Dermot drove off, while Michael joined me and my brother in a hire car. We gave Michael a three-hour tour of Belfast, then dropped him off near a police station. His story was a simple one – a masked man jumped out in front of the lorry, pointed a gun at the windscreen and forced him to stop. Another masked man opened the door to his cab and ordered him out at gunpoint. A third masked man sat in the driving seat of a car behind the lorry. Michael was shoved into the boot, driven round for what seemed like about three hours, ordered out of the boot at gunpoint, given a few slaps and ordered to lie on the side of the road. He waited until the car had driven off, got up and found the police station. What could be simpler?

Dermot took to the narrow country roads around Lough Neagh with his forty-foot lorry and trailer, and duly got stuck in a drain. The lorry, trailer and a hundred grand's worth of TVs and VHS players had to be abandoned.

Back in Belfast, the RUC immediately assumed it was an inside job. Michael was hauled to the notorious interrogation centre in Castlereagh. He cracked like an egg, spilling every last detail about the pre-arranged hijack, fingering me as the ringleader.

That afternoon, my brothers were picked up by the RUC. Simultaneously, a unit called at my home. Refusing to believe that I had gone away for the day, the officers elected to wait for me. When I rang later, my wife had the presence of mind to tell me in code that the police were there at the house. I realised straight away that Michael must have blabbed. The question was, what had he told the RUC? What if he had told them about the IRA's involvement? As ringleader, that would link me directly to the Provies. Armed with this knowledge, wouldn't the RUC just love to get hold of me? God knows what confessions they'd batter out of me. Then there were the Provos, undoubtedly furious that I had roped them into this sorry caper. God knows what they would do to me when they found out. As each horror scenario outflanked the last, I settled on one snap decision: to make a run for it.

For someone in this predicament, there was only one place to go. That evening, I went on the trot to Dundalk. I didn't bother seeking out any of El Paso's fugitives. Instead, I lay low at a farm belonging to an aunt.

I knew I was in the shit. What I didn't know was how deeply I had been dropped in it. Once again, I couldn't see the angles. I decided to ring Andy and Gerry. Perhaps they could get me out of this mess. After all, they had sure helped get me into it.

Of course, Starsky and Hutch had the inside track. They had 'contacts' in the RUC who had put them in the picture.

'Can't you do something?' I demanded. 'I was working for the British government, after all. Can't you talk to someone in the RUC, get the charges dropped?'

'We do that and people start asking why,' said Andy. 'It would blow your cover and you don't want that.'

'No,' I agreed.

'I honestly think you should come back and hand yourself in,' said Andy. 'Just come back and ride it out. You've no previous convictions. You'll probably get a suspended sentence and a fine. We'd pay it for you. When you think about it, this is a great opportunity, really ...'

I was thinking hard, but still not seeing any great opportunities.

Andy carried on. 'The driver, Michael, the one who's talking, he's told the RUC that he thinks the IRA was involved, but he can't say for certain. He says he only dealt with you.'

'Well, that much is true. He did only deal with me.'

'Exactly,' said Andy. 'You come back, hand yourself in, and the IRA will be watching closely to see if you crack under pressure and start naming names. The RUC isn't interested in you, after all. But they'd give you a hell of a good deal if you started naming IRA people. If you don't name any names, the IRA will be impressed. Seriously impressed.'

Of course, he was right. Once again, my handlers had all the answers. Not for the first time, I marvelled at their ability to turn unforeseen circumstances to their advantage. A more cynical person than me might have been suspicious. After all, Andy and Gerry had 'contacts' in the RUC. The RUC was very quick to suspect an inside job. Now I was about to hand myself in – which suited them far more than it suited me.

However, I knew that, if I got the wrong judge on the wrong day, I could end up in the notorious Crumlin Road

Prison in Belfast. 'You're not the first agent this has happened to,' said Andy. 'Look, we've people in prison doing time right now and they're agents. They will not break their cover, and serving time gives them credibility.'

Well, I couldn't stay on the trot forever. Next morning, I walked into the RUC station in Newry.

Local officers couldn't contain their glee. 'Another murdering dog on the way to the Crumlin Road,' said the duty sergeant as he led me across the heavily fortified yard to a heavily fortified van.

I was driven to Musgrave Street Police Station in Belfast. I made a statement naming only those who had already been arrested. I insisted the robbery had nothing to do with the IRA. The terrorism charges were dropped and I was released on bail, charged with theft. I had to answer bail at Newry RUC station every Friday. This would normally have presented no significant challenge to me, but that all changed a fortnight later.

It was about a quarter to seven on a Thursday evening, 28 February 1985, when a series of massive booms ripped through the valley. Cups in our kitchen were still rattling when news of a mortar attack on Newry RUC station came through on the radio.

Piecemeal, the vast scale of the atrocity was revealed. There were believed to be fatalities; the IRA was claiming responsibility; the number of deaths was high because many officers were housed in temporary accommodation; nine RUC officers were dead; two of the dead were women; thirty more were injured, some seriously; it was the single greatest loss of life for the RUC in a single incident.

I knew I had to answer bail at the RUC station the very next day. I felt sick at the prospect of facing them. They would look at me as if I'd set the mortars off myself. How could they know that I was really on their side? Such was the level of mistrust between the agencies that military intelligence would never let the RUC know that I was a double agent, that I was on *their* side, risking *my* life to try and save *their* lives. I went early, wanting to get it over with.

The desk duty officer looked up and shivered with revulsion at the sight of me. 'What the fuck are you doing in here?' he spat.

The shouts started behind him. 'Get that murdering fuck out ... murdering bastard ... IRA scum ... you proud of yourself this morning, eh?'

The abuse soon melded into one vicious torrent of hatred. I was mortified.

From that day on, I got stopped and searched two or three times every day. I returned to the RUC station each Friday to a torrent of filth. Each week, it got more personal, stuff about my family, my wife. I started bringing someone with me to the station, in case it boiled over.

The level of hostility at the RUC station was just starting to wane when the IRA struck again. Five weeks after the attack on the station, on 3 April 1985, a car bomb exploded outside Newry courthouse, killing an RUC officer and a civilian court worker. Once again, the IRA's South Down Command claimed responsibility.

I walked into the RUC station again two days later to answer bail, accompanied by my younger brother. Once again, I ran a gauntlet of abuse, only this time I did so with a smile planted on my face. I had to play the part of an IRA man to the last detail. It was one of the hardest things I'd ever had to do, and I knew that, from that day on, the RUC would make my life in Newry hell.

'I'm getting all this abuse and I'm not even in the IRA,' I complained to a Republican contact.

He was sympathetic, especially as I had named no names and was preparing to take my punishment on the chin. I was terrified of going to jail – not of jail itself, but of the treatment I would receive from IRA prisoners in jail. I had heard harrowing stories of ordinary hooch prisoners being savagely beaten on the wings or being forced to stay in their cells twenty-four hours a day. 'We're political prisoners and you're just a hood,' was the attitude. Then there was my British army past. God knows what unspeakable things would be done to me if the Republican prisoners had a problem with this. I didn't dare think about the consequences of my working for British military intelligence being revealed. It didn't bear thinking about.

My contact at the Republican bar in Newry said he would talk to some of his contacts about it. I decided to stick close to him. He was the only one who could help me on this. Little did I know that sticking close to this man would yield a massive dividend.

I was walking up Hill Street in Newry with him one lunchtime when a man bearing a disturbing resemblance to TV's Roland Rat came scuttling out of the Lido café. He greeted my contact and the pair started chatting like old friends. I hung back a bit, wondering why I had never before set eyes on this man who was acting like my contact's long-lost brother. Suddenly, Roland Rat turned to me and said, 'A friend of yours was asking about you the other day.'

I was racking my brains now, trying to work out what possible connection I might have to this man, hoping not to offend.

'Oh, really?' I smiled, going along with the riddle.

'Oh, yeah,' said Roland, a glint in his eye, 'a friend in Dundalk.'

I felt my cheeks flush.

'You do remember him, don't you?' he said, naming my old nemesis, the IRA's Officer Commanding in Dundalk.

I felt myself panicking. Am I in trouble? Have I been found out?

With that, he burst out laughing. I stayed stony faced. I still couldn't see the funny side to that particular ordeal. This had the effect of cracking him up even more. His bare-faced cheek was starting to irritate me.

'Oh, that wanker,' I said glumly, and that had him laughing even harder.

I shuffled awkwardly, waiting for him to recover from his fit.

'You know, you're all right with me,' said Roland Rat with considerable emphasis, 'especially after that business with the lorry.' With that, he bid farewell to my contact, turned his back on us and set off up Hill Street. He'd gone a few steps when he turned back and said to him, 'Explain to him that I think he's all right, mate,' before scurrying away once more.

'Who the fuck is he?' I asked, still rattled.

'That is Patrick Joseph Blair,' he replied, 'or Mooch as he's better known.'

I nearly spluttered. He didn't need to say any more. I knew all about Mooch, freshly out of prison and freshly reinstated as the IRA's officer commanding in Newry. The recent upsurge in IRA activity around Newry was no coincidence. Mooch was back on the scene. Months earlier, he had finished a long sentence for the attempted murder of a part-time UDR man. The attack was legendary, as reckless as it was ruthless. Mooch and his cohorts waited in a hijacked van for their victim to turn up for work at the water board. The plan was to wait for him to park his car and get out, then shoot him well before he got to the main entrance door. Easy.

Bang on time, the intended target approached the water board's front gate in his car. Mooch cocked his Armalite rifle. One of the team grabbed the handle to the side door, ready to slide it gently open when instructed. The intended target must have had a flash of foreboding. Instead of turning right into the water board, he put his foot down and drove on, at speed. 'Get after him,' came the order and the van roared into life. It took a few minutes to get behind the car. Slowly, the van inched up until they were side by side. The back door of the van was booted open. Boom boom boom, Mooch shot the man repeatedly, hitting him in the head and the body. As the car veered into a fence, the van screeched on.

Miraculously, the man survived. In fact, he recovered

sufficiently to pick Mooch out at a police line-up. Some months later, he attended the court case in a wheelchair.

Oh yes, I knew all about Mooch Blair.

'He's saying you're all right, Kevin,' said my contact.

'How do you mean?' I said, not daring to jump to any conclusions as far as these boys were concerned.

'You're all right. You're not under any suspicion. Mooch thinks you're OK. He'd be happy to work with you.'

'I should think so too,' I said, making out like it was no big deal. Inside, I was doing cartwheels. I floated home. I was all right with the local top IRA man. Clearly, he liked what he had heard about my show of defiance in Dundalk. Maybe he had made his own checks too. For the first time in more than four years of trying, I had finally met the real thing. And he thought I was all right. I was elated.

Andy and Gerry recognised my chance meeting with Mooch as a potentially major breakthrough. I had to find out where Mooch hung out, and I had to engineer further chance meetings with him as soon as possible. I had to get in with him. At the same time, I had to be careful not to push it, not to overdo it, or he would suspect something. I felt I could maintain that balance, right enough.

I discovered that Mooch, unlike a lot of top Provos, did attend the odd Irish night – just long enough to squeeze a bit of flesh and to revel in a bit of adoration. And so, at the next one, I kept my eyes peeled for Mooch Blair.

Eventually, I spotted him holding court near the bar. I slipped through the throng so as to be only a few feet away when he turned round. I pretended I hadn't seen him. 'Ah, you didn't head over to Dundalk tonight then?' came the question, and I turned to see Mooch smiling.

This time I laughed heartily. 'It's Mooch, I believe, isn't it?' I said jovially, offering my right hand.

'It is indeed,' said Mooch, giving my hand a good firm shake, 'and I'm sorry to hear they didn't treat you too well.'

'I was a bit pissed off with them, Mooch, to be honest,' I said. 'I think they thought it was all a big laugh. The poor fella with me pissed himself!'

'The important thing is not to take it seriously,' said Mooch. 'Forget about it.'

The conversation moved swiftly on to my family. People in Newry like to build entire family trees over a drink. To my surprise, carrying on a conversation with Mooch was effortless. We knew the same people. We went to the same schools. I found that I didn't have to think before I spoke.

'We should have a proper chat sometime,' he said finally, as we emptied a second round of drinks. 'You know, somewhere a bit quieter.'

'That'd be great,' I said, and I knew he genuinely meant it. I would be seeing more of Mooch Blair. I was on my way. I had no idea where it would take me, but some sort of odyssey had begun.

I made sure I bumped into Mooch regularly after that. Soon enough, he introduced me to a man with whom I was to become inextricably linked. He was a top IRA figure – unfortunately, I cannot reveal his real name or his true identity here, but I shall call him Conor throughout the book. To my delight, Conor soon sought me out at Irish nights, and we would enjoy a few drinks together. We laughed at the same things, and shared the same interests. Conor even told me he had been in the Territorial Army, where he had developed a lifelong passion for guns and explosives.

Conor made no secret of his IRA career. With his standing and reputation, how could he? He didn't seem very politically motivated, more a man who loved the prestige and power of his position and the buzz of planning operations. For my part, I wasn't remotely politically motivated, and I too loved guns and explosives. It was solid ground on which to construct a murderous friendship. After a few drinks too many, Conor would regale me with his hair-raising escapades as a volunteer. I made no secret of my fascination with his secret life, or of my lust for action since leaving the army. Despite this, he never seemed to get to the point of actively recruiting me into the IRA. I felt constantly like a salesman failing to close the deal.

Meanwhile, our wives hit it off famously and we became a regular social foursome. When Conor had to hotfoot it to Dundalk, my wife and I drove down regularly to see them. A friendship that had at first been cultivated was blossoming naturally. I suppose that sums up the perversity of Northern Ireland. I had more in common with my enemy than with anyone I'd encountered on my side.

Eventually, during the summer of 1985, I felt close enough to Conor to seek a favour. As my November court date for the ill-fated lorry hijack loomed closer, the terror I felt at being sent to prison was making me ill. I confided in Conor my blood-curdling fear that Republican prisoners would target me because of my British army past. He told me he would see what he could do.

Weeks later, Conor told me he had secured certain assurances. If I was sent to prison, no harm would come to me. The relief I felt was indescribable. I had Conor vouching for me, and I had honoured the golden rule of not naming names to the RUC. Finally, after five long years, I was being accepted into the bosom of Republicanism. Now I only hoped that the Crown – for which I had sacrificed so much – would show me mercy.

I thought the court date would never come. I just wanted to get it over with. Finally, one rainy morning in November 1985, my brothers and I set off for Belfast and the Crumlin Road courthouse. We drove in silence along the West Link, past Unity Flats, up the Crumlin Road past the Mater Hospital. We were all thinking the same thing: Would we be making the return journey that evening?

Directly across the road from the courthouse, connected by an underground tunnel, loomed the mock-gothic fortress that is Crumlin Road Prison. Its vast granite walls were encrusted with black filth, making it look more like a grim Victorian factory. I wondered whether I would be sleeping inside those great black walls that night.

Each of us pleaded guilty to the lorry hijack scam. We were all lilywhites, and our solicitor had predicted suspended sentences. He was partially correct.

Brother one got a suspended sentence. Brother two – whom everyone agreed had been dragged into it by me – got eighteen months. Then the judge turned to me. 'Kevin

Fulton, you have pleaded guilty to the charge of theft. It is clear you were the ringleader of this operation, and so you must receive the harshest punishment.'

I closed my eyes.

'I am sentencing you to two years.'

The crack of the gavel was like a shot to the heart. I couldn't even look at my brother as we were led down the steps into separate cells. Paperwork was processed while the shock set like concrete in my veins. I told my solicitor I didn't want to spend Christmas in prison. I wanted to appeal. I'll always remember his words. 'If you appeal, you'll spend the next two Christmases behind bars.'

Next thing, we were being led along a black tunnel, through gate after gate after gate, into a room where I followed the order to hand over all my personal possessions. My brother came in soon after, and the pair of us were led to D-wing, which housed low-risk criminals and just a handful of paramilitaries.

I knew no one was going to unlock the cell door and let me out, so I decided to get my head down and get on with it. If I behaved myself, I would be out in twelve months. I could just about get my head around a 365-day countdown. God alone knows how anybody copes at the start of a ten-year sentence. In the meantime, I had weekly visits to look forward to and, providing I kept out of trouble, a week's parole in six months.

I coped with the day-to-day routine well. I was a starman – slang for an inmate serving his first prison sentence – and so my good behaviour was swiftly rewarded with privileges. I got a prized job in the laundry room. It was easy work but the real benefit was it had its own toilet. I was the only prisoner in Crumlin Road Prison able to take a shit in peace. Daily I saw the dehumanising effect prison was having on my fellow inmates, and I clung to this single privilege.

At night, out of my cell window, I could see the lights of a flourmill and I could hear the noises and smell the smells of Belfast. Believe me, this is far better than staring at a wall. Another D-wing privilege was that we were allowed to keep a radio in our cell. This was my lifeline to the outside world. To refer to these small mercies as privileges in the outside world seems laughable. Trust me, in prison, they're worth more than gold.

It became apparent very quickly that I wouldn't be getting any grief from the Republican prisoners. Indeed, I made a point of befriending any I could. I realised that I could achieve one thing in prison – I could enhance my credibility with the Provisional IRA. And never did boosting my credibility with the IRA seem such a good idea. What also became apparent very quickly was that the screws locked and unlocked the doors, but that was as far as their powers went. In Crumlin Road Prison, the IRA controlled everything.

Two events in particular boosted my reputation with Republican prisoners. The first was a surprise visit by Conor's wife. Of course, I desperately looked forward to my wife's weekly visits, but they broke my heart. I felt overwhelmed with guilt. My poor wife hadn't chosen to get embroiled in this Dirty War. My life was one huge lie and now she was paying the price. Every visit took place within earshot of a dozen screws, making normal conversation impossible. It was almost a relief when Conor's wife turned up in her place. Word quickly spread around the prison – Fulton's so tight with Conor he sent his missus to visit him!

The second major boost to my kudos happened in March 1986. All low-grade inmates were being vetted for transfer to the newly built Maghaberry Prison in Antrim. The facilities there were top notch, and anything had to be better than crumbling Crumlin Road. Everyone was desperate to go. I had served four months with exemplary behaviour, so I saw my transfer to Maghaberry as a formality. Again, in prison, something as trivial as a transfer takes on a wildly exaggerated significance. So, when my brother got the transfer and I didn't, I was enraged.

To make matters worse, my brother was going to be allowed out on parole every other weekend. I couldn't understand it. Far more dangerous prisoners than me were being rewarded with the transfer to Maghaberry. Why wasn't I?

I stormed down to Alex Flanagan, the prison censor, and demanded an explanation.

'Sorry, kid,' said Alex, 'you're here for the stay.'

'What?' I demanded.

'They won't give you security clearance,' said Alex.

'Why not? I've worked hard. I've stayed out of trouble.'

'In confidence, Kevin,' said Alex, his outstretched hands willing me to calm down, 'it's your reports. You're a suspected paramilitary. It's the, er, company you've been keeping.'

Yet again, everyone had me in the IRA. Except the IRA. I made sure word got round as to why I had been refused a transfer. I was working hard for Andy and Gerry. What worried me was that they hadn't had the decency even to get in touch with me since my conviction. I knew they couldn't visit me directly, but I thought they'd have the connections and the clout to get to me somehow. Surely they could send someone on a 'legal' visit, just to keep me informed. I didn't dare ring the 830512 number from prison. I assumed all calls were traced or recorded in some way. I started to feel desperately alone and cut off. I began to wonder if I'd been dropped. Would they still be on the 830512 number when I got out? Prison's real punishment is giving you too much time to think. Nights are the hardest. Worst-case scenarios creep up on you during the day but you can beat them away. They come back and torment you at night. There is nothing to fill those great black voids of night except worry. I needed some certainties in my life. I craved reassurance. I was getting neither from my handlers.

Finally, in July 1986, the morning of my week's parole arrived. I met my wife outside, then headed straight to a coin box to ring my handlers. I was desperate for a meeting, desperate to know where they had been and what was going on. Andy came to the phone, eventually. He was so casual you'd think I'd just been away for a piss.

'Glad to hear you're all right,' he said. 'I'll get back to you later and we'll arrange a meet some time this week.'

I was painting the bedroom ceiling at home the following day when the phone rang. It was my mother. They were expecting me for dinner. 'Don't be coming down town to see us,' she said.

'What?' I said.

'Just don't be coming down town. Three policemen have been shot.'

Next thing, it was on the news: three RUC men shot dead in Market Street. They were parked up in an armoured car eating ice cream when a gunman approached the vehicle and opened fire. The image made me shudder – the innocent pleasure of eating ice cream juxtaposed with such cold-blooded and barbaric murder. No doubt, they would be cracking sick gags about it in some bar in Dundalk.

The phone rang again. It was Andy. 'Listen, Kevin, I'm afraid we won't be meeting you now.'

'What?'

'We've a lot going on with the three policemen,' he said. 'People are watching, too many people.' He clearly sensed my disappointment. 'It's for your own good,' he said. 'It's best for your safety at this stage.'

'There's a few things we really need to talk about,' I said.

'Trust me, it's for the greater good, Kevin. We've got to think about the bigger picture. You're coming to the stage now where you're nearly in. We're not going to let anything get in the way of that.'

He hung up and I suddenly realised a terrifying truth. I now needed Andy and Gerry more than they needed me. They were the only people on the planet who knew the truth about my life. They were the only people on the planet with whom I could truly be myself. With everyone else – my wife, my parents, my best friends – I had to remember my lines. I had to be careful not to slip up. I had to live the lie. Without

Andy and Gerry, the past five years – all the risks, all the sacrifices – meant nothing. I relied on them for money. I relied on them for making my decisions for me. I would rely on them if it all went wrong.

They had been in charge of my life for so long now that I felt incapable of surviving without them. My life was literally in their hands.

And I liked it like that.

CHAPTER FOUR

I got out of prison in November 1986 and immediately sought a meeting with my handlers. After a year in limbo, I needed certainties in my life. I was desperate to know whether or not my arrangement with military intelligence still stood. A year is a long time, particularly when you haven't even heard from your employers. By now, I had a criminal record and was officially suspected of IRA membership. Alternative career prospects – previously rare – now seemed non-existent. I couldn't think of any other legal way to make a living.

Andy and Gerry greeted me like a long-lost brother. They assured me that our working relationship had never ceased and handed me a lump sum to that effect. They apologised for not making contact, insisting it was simply too dangerous. They said they had been keeping tabs on my progress courtesy of 'contacts' within the prison, and that I'd played a blinder! After a year of uncertainty, this was exactly what I needed to hear.

Andy and Gerry were particularly excited about my burgeoning friendship with Conor. They told me not to bother any more with my previous contacts and the Newry corner boys. Conor was my dream ticket. He was my key into the IRA. Conor was also my ticket back to El Paso.

The next day, I took up an invitation to visit him at his new home in Dundalk. My fear of Dundalk and its desperadoes held sway no more. Prison had given me credibility. I had passed a crucial test: I had served my time; I had named no names; I was in the club. There would be no shakedowns this time, especially as I had found out that my former tormentor-in-chief in Dundalk had been discharged from the IRA in disgrace. According to the whispers in prison, during a particularly raucous Republican piss-up in Dundalk, he was accused of getting in trouble with another IRA man's wife. The woman's husband said, if the IRA didn't boot him out, he'd shoot him. Despite his status as officer commanding in Dundalk, the man was exiled to Dublin. I was returning to Dundalk on my own terms, as the honoured guest of a leading IRA figure.

Conor was sharing a house on Thomas Street with Niall who, though still in his twenties, had exhibited sufficient bloodlust to be regarded as something of an IRA legend. Conor told me Niall was on the run for murder – again. In his short but spectacular IRA career, Niall – who had close relatives in the highest echelons of the Provos – had stiffed anything from four to ten people, depending on which local bar-room estimate you cared to believe. I had no doubt that four was leaning on the conservative side. I also had no doubt that Conor had been knee-deep in the mortar attack on Newry RUC station. And so I shared my evening drinking and having the craic with a pair of killers.

It was my way of saying thanks to Conor for all he had done. He had proven himself a good friend while I'd been inside. It was a friendship I needed so I chose not to dwell on Conor's motivation for taking me under his wing. At least not yet. Conor was my friend, Niall was my friend. That led to introductions to some of the Provisional IRA's major players in Dundalk. I met Leonard Hardy, or Hardbap as he was known, a Belfast Provo wanted for questioning for a whole range of bombing offences. His common-law wife was Donna Maguire, who would later be arrested for terrorist offences on the continent. I met James Morgan, who had served time for possession of explosives in 1984. I met Tony Hughes, who survived being shot in the neck during an SAS ambush and was on the run. I met Dermot Finucane, also on the run after escaping from the Maze Prison in Belfast. A few years later, his brother Pat, a solicitor, would be shot dead in front of his wife and children by, it is now generally thought, Loyalists colluding with the British army's Force Research Unit.

I quickly picked up on two general trends amongst these men. The first: Belfast Provos thought that anyone from outside Belfast was a bit thick. The second: all these men suspected each other of being a tout. Paranoia ruled supreme.

I'm sure they suspected me too, but it didn't matter. With Conor vouching for me, I was becoming one of them. I was on my way.

My handlers agreed, and by now they had worked out a way to further enhance my 'usefulness' to Conor and to the IRA in Dundalk.

'We need to get you back to work,' said Andy, 'and we've thought of just the thing.'

Gerry took up the thread. 'We've thought of the perfect job for you. Or at least the perfect job for you as far as Conor and the IRA might be concerned. Flexible hours, good money, lots of freedom of movement.'

'So?' I said expectantly.

'We want you to buy an ice-cream van,' said Andy.

'Right,' I smiled, waiting for some sort of punch line.

'We're serious,' said Gerry. 'It'll work really well. Trust us.'

For the life of me, I couldn't see how Kevin Fulton flogging lollies out of a van window would tilt the balance of the Dirty War in our favour, but they were insistent. They had sourced an ice-cream van for sale, asking price £1500. I thought the least British intelligence could do was pay for it, but no.

'You'll have to borrow the money from the credit union,' said Andy, 'in case the IRA starts asking questions.' A credit union is a co-operative bank owned and run by its members. For someone with my chequered employment history, it was the only way to secure a low-interest loan.

'Why would the IRA start asking questions about an ice-cream van?' I asked.

I soon found out why. Above the van's windscreen was a compartment containing a fluorescent sign in the shape of an ice-cream cone. By the time Andy and Gerry had finished their handiwork, the compartment also contained a hidden video camera, operated by a remote-control panel tucked under the window hatch.

In the back of the van, under a fixed Formica cover, they had discovered a secret compartment. Clearly, the previous Mr Whippy had indulged in a little cross-border smuggling. Andy and Gerry suggested I show this secret compartment to Conor at the first opportunity. In the meantime, they would set about securing me a special trading licence so I could sell ice cream north and south of the border.

I quickly realised that acquiring this licence was a tactical masterstroke. Conor immediately spotted the opportunities. Within days, I was running 'coms' for him, to and fro across the border. A 'com' is an important IRA communication, written in microscopic handwriting on a single Rizla cigarette paper. It is then wrapped in cling film and rolled into a tiny ball. Despite the march of technology – or perhaps because of it – coms were still the preferred method of communication between IRA units of command. For one thing, it's secure – you can easily tell if a com has been opened and resealed. In the event of a raid or an arrest, a com can be swallowed in an instant; and, if need be, it can be covertly transferred to a third party – preferably someone of the opposite sex – by a kiss on the lips!

My handlers decided against intercepting these messages. In their view, winning Conor's total trust was my priority. If transporting the coms was a test, I passed it with honours, and the nature of my hidden carriage soon became much more substantial.

I remember the hot summer morning in 1987 when Conor handed me a weighty package, wrapped in thick brown paper and gaffer tape. He asked me to deliver it to a garage in Newry. He watched as I secreted the package into the van's hidden compartment and set off. I stopped two miles short of the border, clambered into the back, yanked up the Formica partition, took out the mystery parcel and gently peeled back the wrapping. It was a battery pack. I suspected it was designed for one thing only – to detonate a bomb. By transporting this battery pack to its destination, I dreaded that I might be playing an active and vital role in an IRA bomb plot – a plot that would most likely cause injury and/or death. I was committed to it now – failing to make the delivery would leave me vulnerable – so I followed Conor's instructions to the letter.

However, this latest advancement in my IRA career opened my eyes to the moral dilemma at the root of my new life. The following Wednesday, I challenged my handlers about the morality of moving tools of death for a terrorist organisation. Did we really want to be assisting the IRA in its murderous activities? They were pragmatic – if I didn't smuggle the battery pack up north, somebody else would. At least when I made the delivery, they knew exactly where it was going.

They assured me that my information was helping the security forces second-guess bombings and shootings. As such, my work was saving lives. That made me feel about ten feet tall – until I considered the potential consequences. Usually, there were only three parties privy to my smuggling activities – Conor, the recipient of the delivery and me.

'Supposing you act on some of my information and stop a bombing or a shooting. Won't it be obvious that the information must have come from me?' I asked them.

'We'd never, ever leave you exposed like that,' said Gerry. 'Your position within the IRA is more important to us than anything else.'

'More important than saving the lives of civilians?' I asked. 'Are you saying you'd let a member of the public die rather than compromise my position?'

'I could never admit to something like that,' Gerry said, shifting awkwardly. 'Let's just say we judge every operation on its merits. Clearly, if they're planning a massive bomb that's going to kill a lot of innocent people, then we'd have to do something to stop it. That's when we'd pull you out.'

It was harder than ever to see the angles. I decided I had no choice but to trust Andy and Gerry. They had the intelligence, the resources and the experience necessary to see the angles. My life depended on it.

By now, in my capacity as Conor's courier, I was getting involved in what Andy and Gerry would call Grade One activity. My next special delivery was a revolver that Conor wanted delivered to First Avenue in Newry. He asked me if I was feeling bold enough to risk smuggling a gun over the border.

'Only too happy to oblige,' I replied cockily, and Conor applauded my steely nerve.

'You've got balls, I'll say that for ya,' he said.

How was he to know that I had nothing to fear? I waltzed through unchecked, and that night, as instructed, I hid the revolver in a hedgerow near the home of IRA man Sean Mathers. I would soon get to know Sean Mathers, and put him behind bars.

Throughout 1987, I crossed the border unchallenged, with bags of fertiliser, guns, shotgun cartridges, bullets and battery packs. There was hardly any time left to sell ice cream. When I did get round to it, I was pleasantly surprised by just how profitable an enterprise it was. So profitable that my sudden arrival raised the ire of other ice-cream sellers.

On one particular day, I was handing a brace of 99s to a young kid in a village when a rival ice-cream seller neglected to knock on the side entrance door of the van before stomping in. 'What the fuck are you doing?' he shouted.

He lumbered towards me until his face was an inch from mine. 'Get the fuck off our patch and stay off,' he said. I could tell he meant it. There would be no more 99s sold that night. He needn't have bothered. I was going to leave anyway.

That night, I dropped in on Conor and told him about my hostile reception.

'Don't worry,' said Conor. 'I'll sort that out for you.'

A few days later, Conor told me I'd be having no more trouble from this particular person. Apparently, two IRA men had called at their home for a 'chat'. After that, they didn't so much as cast a glance in my direction. I'm ashamed to admit it, but I enjoyed calling in such protection. I didn't see why they should have a divine right to be the sole purveyors of ice cream in my local area, and I wasn't about to be intimidated off my own streets.

My triumph spurred me on. I expanded my operations all over the North and as far south as Dublin. To boost my income, I hired pitches at major events like rock concerts, football matches and agricultural shows. My decision to sell ice cream at an air show presented me with my first real scare as a double agent.

I had paid for a pitch at the Aldergrove Air Show in Belfast. I made the mistake of mentioning this to Conor, whose eyes lit up. A few days later, he pulled me to one side and said, 'Would you take a bomb in?'

'What? Where?'

'Into the air show at Aldergrove?'

I tried not to look horrified. I just about managed to squeeze out an 'I'll think about it'.

First chance I got, I rang my handlers, who were similarly knocked sideways by the plan.

'You must put him off,' said Andy.

'How?' I said.

'Tell him it's too dangerous.'

Conor, though, had already planned it all out. I would smuggle a Semtex bomb into the show in my secret compartment. I would then wait for the coded signal to pass the device over to an IRA operative. Conor had even worked out what this coded signal would be. A man would come up and ask for a 'slider', which is a block of ice cream between two wafers. Now, of course, I didn't sell sliders, I only sold cones, so this would be how I would know. I would pass the bomb over, get out of the van and walk away as swiftly as possible. The plan seemed preposterous. I didn't know whether to laugh or cry.

'Supposing someone else comes up and asks for a slider?' I said to Conor. 'They'd be in for a fucking shock, wouldn't they?'

'You'll know the man all right,' said Conor. 'Look, it's too good an opportunity to miss. Imagine if we blow up an army chopper or an army plane! Think about the publicity!'

I hadn't been asked to do anything of this magnitude before. I had to appear willing. Maybe it was another test. And so, as the date of the air show approached, Conor got more excited and I got less sleep.

I demanded some guarantees from my handlers. Surely if Conor insisted on proceeding with this plan, they'd have to pull me out.

They seemed unmoved by my predicament. 'Tell him the security will be too tight,' said Andy. 'Tell him whatever you have to tell him, just make sure he doesn't go ahead with this plan!'

Eventually, I plucked up the courage to express my disquiet to Conor about his ambitious plot. 'I was on the phone to one of the guys in the office at the air show yesterday,' I started, trying to sound as nonchalant as possible. 'He's a helpful young fella. Anyways, he happened to mention that the army plans to search every vehicle going in. I think it's too risky.'

Conor took a deep breath before deciding how to react.

'Yeah, you're right,' said Conor, just like that. 'It's too risky.' And that was that. As quickly as it had flashed into his mind, his elaborate plans for an atrocity were dissolved. Perhaps it was a test after all. Had I passed?

A week later, I drove my ice-cream van into the Aldergrove Air Show and located my pitch. It was tucked away in a rear corner of the field – useless for selling ice cream, but the best possible position to carry out a bomb attack. Pitched right next to me were six Ulster Defence Regiment recruitment tents. Nobody searched me or my van going in. I didn't mention any of this to my tutor-in-terror, Conor.

By mid-1987, Conor and I were inseparable, and with good reason. Conor couldn't drive, and so I became a sort of unofficial chauffeur. He had very little money and no source of income, so I let him help me out on my ice-cream rounds in the Republic, and I secured him odd jobs, decorating for friends and relatives. For much of 1987, army intelligence was putting food on Conor's table, courtesy of me.

He was grateful. He showed his gratitude by involving me in his primary IRA activity – building bombs. By the end of 1987, I was running guns, I was assisting in bomb-building and I was getting to know major IRA operatives. In short, I was doing more for the Provisional IRA than most of the organisation's official members. Or, as Conor put it, I was doing too much.

A new directive had been issued by IRA leadership: anybody working for the IRA, in any capacity, had to be 'green-booked'. The Green Book was the official IRA constitution and code of practice. Once you were green-booked, you became subject to the IRA's own 'rules'. From the IRA's perspective, there was sound logic behind this directive. Under the rules of the Green Book, suspected informants or double agents could be investigated, tried and executed by the IRA's internal security. The leadership assumed that this homicidal proviso would deter any would-be informants from infiltrating the IRA.

Unsurprisingly, I wasn't in a desperate hurry to be green-booked. I didn't fancy subscribing to the IRA's concept of justice – a kangaroo court followed by one behind the ear. However, that wasn't my major concern. After all, I knew they'd kill me if they found out who I was working for – green-booked or not.

My gravest concern was that I would become a servant to the IRA and its leadership. I would be an IRA subject. I would have to follow orders from faceless, nameless IRA chiefs, unquestioningly. I liked the current arrangement, dealing exclusively with Conor. Take the Aldergrove Air Show incident. Had I been ordered from on high to smuggle a bomb in, how could I have refused without inviting the attentions of internal security? At least with Conor I was dealing with a friend. I could appeal to his common sense. I could protect myself.

I told Conor I liked just dealing with him. 'I'm not sure I trust anyone else in the organisation yet,' I said.

'Well, you'll still be working with me,' said Conor. 'The thing is, if you don't get green-booked, I won't be able to work with you any more. It's up to you.'

I didn't see any way around it. Of course, my handlers

were cock-a-hoop at the prospect. 'We've waited nearly seven years for this,' said Gerry. 'I think we should celebrate!'

Days later, Conor told me the arrangements had been made. I already knew about the process. One night a week, for about six weeks, I would have to attend a one-to-one tutorial where I'd be taught about Irish history and politics. The whole complicated mess would be explained to me – the 1916 rebellion, Irish parliaments recognised by the IRA and Irish parliaments not recognised by the IRA – all from a rabid Republican perspective, of course. I feared I would find their historical justifications for the mindless slaughter of innocent people hard to swallow. I dreaded it.

Up until now, I had got away with saying I wanted to join the IRA because I loved guns and bombs. That was my cover, my way of avoiding difficult ideological discussions about crushing the systems of British imperialism and fighting for a united Ireland. I might have been in character as Kevin Fulton, IRA terrorist, but for me to start spouting this stuff would require an Oscar-winning performance, which I knew I didn't have in me. It's one thing to join a terrorist organisation, it's entirely another to pretend you subscribe to its aims.

Then I learned that my tutor was to be Niall. What a relief! If ever I'd met an IRA man without a scintilla of ideology, it was Niall. He was in it for the power and the buzz, nothing else. At least I wouldn't have to feign any political or sociological motivation with him. He was a friend. He knew I was made of the right stuff.

I turned up for my first tutorial totally at ease.

'Why do you want to join the IRA?' said Niall, opening things up. 'And don't tell me it's because you like shooting people and blowing things up!'

'Because I like shooting people and blowing things up,' I smiled.

'Look, I know you're suitable. You're as good as in,' said Niall, 'but we've got to go through the motions.'

'OK,' I said, and we understood each other perfectly.

As the tutorials ground on, Niall did help me come to one alarming conclusion about my new life inside the Provisional IRA. 'You know,' he said, his earnest tone earning my full attention, 'all the IRA can offer you is heartache. It's a shit life, being a volunteer. You go to prison. Your loved ones go through hell. You lose friends. You lose loved ones. All the time you're half-expecting to be arrested, or blown up, or shot. If the army or the police or the Orangemen don't get you, the stress will. You know I've had two heart attacks?'

'What?'

'I've had two heart attacks and I'm not yet thirty. I mean, are you sure you want all the grief?'

Niall's plaintive and touching little speech brought into sharp focus the enormity of what I was taking on. I suddenly found it hard to see a way out of this alive, or at least alive and healthy. All I ever wanted was to be a British soldier. Now I was signing up to a doctrine that made me the enemy of the British army, the RUC and the Ulster Defence Regiment. None of these organisations had the slightest idea that I was really on their side. My handlers wouldn't be able to protect me from them.

It was 1988 and the greatest threat to my life would now come from my own colleagues in the British army. In recent years, the SAS had seemingly adopted a shoot-to-kill policy with regard to IRA members, armed or not. (And rightly so, in my opinion.) There had been numerous occasions when they had opened fire on unarmed IRA members.

Less than a year earlier, in May 1987, the SAS intercepted an IRA unit on its way to attack the RUC station in Loughgall, County Armagh, and shot eight of them dead. If I was there, I would have been shot dead too. How could my handlers protect me from the SAS?

Then there was the risk from Protestant paramilitary groups, every bit as proficient in the art of slaughter as the IRA.

To cap it all, there was the ever-present danger that the IRA would discover my role as a special agent. Now I'd been green-booked, the IRA had a licence to act as judge, jury and executioner if I was suspected of being a tout. And there were so many ways I could see this happening.

If the security forces used my information to thwart IRA attacks, then surely it would only be a matter of time before my new IRA colleagues would conclude that I was working for the other side. As a fully fledged IRA member, sooner or later I would be ordered to pull a trigger or to plant a bomb. To refuse would blow my cover and bring instant death. What was the alternative? To kill on the IRA's behalf would make me a terrorist and a murderer. How could my handlers protect me from this predicament?

In short, I didn't have just one half of the warring factions to worry about – I was taking on the whole bloody lot. And, as Niall reminded me, if they don't get you, the heart attacks will.

Welcome to the Provisional IRA.

My terror at being called upon to attack my own side materialised almost immediately.

By now, Leonard Hardy – Hardbap – had risen to the rank of OC in Newry. He started asking me about my time in Berlin with the British army. Soon he made it clear he was trying to establish the feasibility of launching terrorist attacks in Germany. He told me that the IRA had an active service unit there that had launched some successful operations in the early eighties. The Belfast hierarchy felt it was time to resume the campaign in mainland Europe. Would I be willing to discuss what I knew, in confidence, with two senior IRA men?

How could I say no? As instructed, I waited in the lobby of a country-house hotel just outside Dublin for the two men to arrive. They were easy to spot. In his dapper cream suit, reading spectacles and pipe, the elder of the two men cut a statesman-like dash. The other man, squat and scruffy in an old parka coat, looked like a farm labourer.

The older man immediately took charge. He was well spoken with a slight Belfast lilt. I never did find out exactly who he was. He asked me all about Berlin and the squaddies' routine. He asked me what I thought would make a good target. I told him that the brigadier in overall command of the British forces in Berlin would be the most high profile and, ironically, the easiest target of all. I told him how the brigadier lived in an unfortified home on Herr Strasse, guarded by one solitary unarmed police officer. Across the road, the Grünewald forest offered perfect cover for a sniper.

I had an equally good plan for an attack on British squaddies. I told them that squaddies were most vulnerable when they were on rest-and-recreation trips in the mountains. The army regularly block-booked forty soldiers into a *Staatsbad* resort – a superior resort that offers curative spa waters – in the spa town of Bad Reichenhall in the Bavarian Alps of southern Germany.

The pair looked impressed. They told me I would be hearing from them.

'I trust you haven't discussed this meeting with anyone other than Mr Hardy?' said the older man.

'Of course not,' I said, cursing myself for telling Conor about it.

'Good. Let's keep it that way. Do not discuss what went on here today with another soul.'

A week later, Hardbap told me he had been instructed from on high to 'wrap me in cotton wool' until further notice. A month later, I met the two gentlemen again. One handed me £2,000 and told me to carry out reconnaissance on the brigadier's accommodation and the spa resort for possible attacks. I was instructed which route to take and which modes of transport to use. One point they laboured repeatedly: if you think you're being followed, abandon the mission. Once again, I was ordered not to discuss the trip with anyone other than Hardbap. I comforted myself with the knowledge that Conor and my handlers were the only other people privy to this plan.

Andy and Gerry told me to go along with the scheme, and so, in September 1988, I took the ferry from Rosslare to Le Havre. I disembarked in France and took a complimentary bus to the train station. By the time I spotted the temporary passport booth that had been set up along the route, it was too late to turn back.

The three men stationed at the booth were straight out of film noir. Each sported a trench coat, a fedora and a languid, world-weary pose. They cast cursory glances at the passports held under their noses – at least until mine was presented. After a thirty-second inspection, the studious man in the booth stamped my passport and then nodded very obviously to one of the other men. I felt like I was starring in a low-budget Cold War spy caper.

Unnerved, I walked speedily to the bus. As I climbed aboard, a man got on right behind me. I noticed his hand on the handrail. Half of his index finger was missing. 'Excuse me, sir,' he said in a French accent, 'I don't mean to cause you alarm but one of the men from the passport booth is following you.' Over his shoulder, I twigged one of the Philip Marlowe lookalikes bustling my way, his trench coat flapping in the breeze. I decided to sit at the back so I could keep an eye on him.

Marlowe read *L'Equipe* all the way to the Gare du Nord station in Paris. He didn't look round once. He did follow me off the bus, though. If these boys were trying to be covert, I remember thinking, they weren't doing a very good job. The next stage of my journey was to catch a train from the Gare de L'Est train station in Paris to Berlin. As I walked from the Gare du Nord to the Gare de L'Est, I noticed Marlowe in pursuit. I turned a corner, my mind racing. Who the fuck is this guy? I decided to stop and turn round so that I would be waiting for Marlowe when he rounded the corner. Imagine my surprise when two people strode purposefully towards me. On seeing me standing there facing them, the pair visibly recoiled, shuffling clumsily over to a shop window. Had I not had a train to catch, I would have confronted them.

I marched on and noticed a man in similar dress in front of me. I could have sworn there were two more watching me from a pavement café. Everywhere I looked lurked another Marlowe.

I walked round the building a second time. As I passed the entrance, I saw a large, mysterious Citroën car with blacked-out windows and three chunky aerials jutting from the roof. The Marlowes were still in hot pursuit. I had been advised to abandon the entire mission if I spotted anything suspicious. In my book, being pursued by half a dozen men in trench coats and fedoras qualified as suspicious. I stopped at a stationery store and bought an envelope and some postage stamps. I placed my train tickets to Berlin in the envelope, sealed it, scrawled my mother-in-law's address on the front, stuck on the stamps and plopped it into a letterbox.

I then hailed a taxi and jumped in. 'Take me to an airport with flights to the Irish Republic,' I said.

'*Pardon?*' the driver said with more than a hint of disdain.

'Take me to the fucking airport, now!' I spat the words out and he knew I was in no mood for games.

The two Marlowes jumped into the mysterious blacked-out Citroen and followed. When we got to Charles De Gaulle Airport, they were still on my tail. I paid the driver and walked to the Aer Lingus sales desk, the two Marlowes following diligently. The earliest available flight to Dublin was early the following morning. As I paid, I took the time to steal a really good look at my pursuers. They were tanned, well groomed and very French. What I couldn't understand was why they were being so obvious, so blatant. As I headed to the airport hotel, I gave them a hearty wave and a smile. They just stared.

The next morning, they were waiting for me in reception. They shadowed me all the way to the departure gate. I waved farewell again and wondered what the fuck was going on. Who were these men?

Only Hardbap, the two men from Belfast, Conor and my handlers knew about this trip. Whoever was following me must have been in cahoots with one, some or all of these people. My handlers insisted it was nothing to do with them and I believed them. They had nothing to gain. I showed Hardbap my stamped passport, the tickets and the receipts and he seemed genuinely perplexed and perturbed, as he would have to explain the abandoned mission to IRA chiefs. He had nothing to gain.

That left Conor. Of course, I couldn't tell anyone that I had told Conor about my trip. I'd been green-booked and such a breach of discipline could cause me real problems. It would remain a secret between Conor and me.

I knew I could count on Conor. We were bonded by shared

secrets. It was around this time, after a few beers too many, that he revealed a dark secret to me. Conor told me he had been involved in the shooting of the three ice-cream-eating RUC officers in Market Street, Newry, when I had been on parole the previous summer.

The dead men were Charles Allen, Peter Kilpatrick and Karl Blackbourne. Their killers were dressed as butchers, and the killings are known in Newry as the 'butcher murders'. Conor told me he went to the front passenger side and shot one of the men. He said the young guy in the back was calling for his mum. He gave the young officer the chance to go for his gun, but he made no attempt, so Conor shot him.

The horror didn't end there. To add further insult to the police and the memory of their fallen colleagues, Conor left a sick calling card at the scene. Police have always believed that the unexploded grenade found in the car had been faulty. That's why it failed to go off. The truth is much more twisted than that. Conor claimed he had deliberately tampered with the Russian hand grenade so that it wouldn't detonate. However, he made sure it looked live and ready to go off at any second. This prevented the security forces from removing the three bodies from the scene until bomb-disposal experts could confirm that the area was safe. As a result, they lay there in full public view for hours.

Conor said the motive was revenge. Two months earlier, an IRA man called Seamus McElwaine had been shot dead by the SAS near the Fermanagh border. His body was left lying in the open for hours because security forces said they had to make the area safe before moving in. Republicans were outraged.

The hand-grenade stunt was a message to the security forces. It brought home to me Conor's ruthless potential. It was also a vital connection to Conor. By letting me in on his dark secret, he had let me in to his world.

CHAPTER FIVE

By 1988, I felt I had made it into the inner sanctum of the IRA, albeit in a lowly capacity. I was considered the sorcerer's apprentice – Conor's bright new trainee in the art of bomb-making.

Conor was the leader of a small team of volunteers in Dundalk who devoted themselves to the construction and the development of bombs. By all accounts, Conor was one of the IRA's most skilful and prolific bomb-makers. They came to him from all over the six counties for 'squibs' – slang for bombs. Like a proud craftsman, he began painstakingly deconstructing his art for my benefit. He wanted me to learn the trade because, according to Conor, the IRA needed more bomb-makers.

It was literally a dying art. Historically, bombers were supplied with devices but made their own timers, usually using second-hand clocks or watches. Mistakes were made and the cost a heavy one. Increasingly, volunteers were being killed by their own devices. In a bid to counter these costly blunders, the IRA introduced strict new rules about how bombs and timers should be made and distributed. Bombs had to be constructed properly by a recognised IRA bomb-maker. Box timers had to be professionally produced in a secret factory unit. Basically, the IRA had decided to take the DIY out of the incendiary.

From the mid-eighties on, ready-made bombs with professionally made box timers were delivered to bombers. Box timers were designed to be idiot-proof – anyone could use one. Often, this was the only skill the actual planter of the bomb brought to the operation – you could plant a bomb and have no knowledge of its contents or its likely impact. All the actual planter of the bomb had to do was set the timer and get the hell away from there as quickly and as inconspicuously as possible.

As a result, anyone could plant a bomb. But very few IRA men actually knew how to construct a bomb. Mixing explosives had become a highly prized secret skill within the IRA. I was about to become privy to this black art. First, I started with the simple stuff.

Like any apprentice or trainee, I had to prove my dedication to my new trade by accepting the most lowly and demeaning tasks without complaint. After the hi-jinks in Germany, 1988 saw me literally getting back to the grind. I was set the task of grinding garden fertiliser pellets down to dust. Powdered fertiliser was a key component in IRA bombs, so I got grinding. The fertiliser could only be bought in the Republic – in the North, it was coated in plastic to ensure it couldn't be ground down. One bag, costing about a fiver, was enough to take down any medium-sized building – once it had been turned into dust.

The most effective way of turning ammonium-nitrate fertiliser into dust was to painstakingly crush the stuff, in a coffee grinder. On my trips down south to buy bags of fertiliser, I was always on the lookout for big old-fashioned coffee grinders, the Bewley's model being the most sought after. Inevitably, coffee houses had an old grinder dumped out the back in decent working order but superseded some time since by a smaller, smarter model. Café owners were baffled by my offer to purchase their old grinders. I would spin them some tall tale about being a mature chemistry student, studying developments in coffee production, or some such rubbish. In the end, they would insist on giving the grinder to me for nothing. 'Sure, you're almost doing me a favour taking it away!' Bless their naïve souls.

When used to crush chemical matter as opposed to coffee beans, a grinder lasted a matter of days before literally grinding to a halt, the fertiliser rotting away the parts. A fresh grinder had to be found somehow. Cue a spate of armed robberies on cafés and coffee shops. Perplexed café owners told police that the thieves got away with their takings *and* their coffee grinder. 'What would they want with a coffee grinder?' they would ask in exasperation. They were always shocked to hear of its deadly alternative function.

Once acquired, the grinder and myself were spirited to

some draughty tumbledown farmhouse in a God-forsaken backwater of County Louth, and I got to work. I remember the day when I finally squeezed out enough pyrotechnic powder for a bomb. Conor arrived with his toolbox and set to work. He constructed the device in my presence, like some deranged TV chef, explaining the role and function of each component part as he went along. His passion for the minute mechanics of the device seemed to distract him from the single, terrifying reality of our handiwork – we were building a bomb that could kill and maim.

When I told Conor I didn't like the idea of hurting or killing innocent people, he assured me that commercial property would be this bomb's only victim. For reasons I could never understand, crippling Northern Ireland's economy remained a staple IRA objective. To my intense frustration, he refused to tell me anything else, insisting that it was for my own good. So I was able to tell my handlers that a major explosion was imminent, but that was as far as it went. I couldn't tell them when and I couldn't tell them where. For days, I lived in gut-wrenching dread that my handiwork would injure, maim or kill.

When I finally learned of the catastrophic fruits of my labours, I was stunned. The bomb had literally flattened a massive warehouse in Belfast. To my immense relief there had been no casualties. It had been detonated in the middle of the night, after a warning.

However, as I was all too aware, the IRA wasn't always so public spirited. The previous November, during the annual Remembrance Sunday ceremony in Enniskillen, County

Fermanagh, an IRA bomb slaughtered eleven innocent people and injured sixty-three. All these people were doing was remembering British soldiers – Protestant and Catholic – who had sacrificed their lives to fight fascism. IRA bombs would do worse in the future, and I was still grinding out explosive powder. What if one of my bombs caused an Enniskillen? I wanted my handlers to tell me how I was supposed to live with that.

By now, Andy had moved on. Gerry's new partner was a man called Alan. It didn't matter who I got it from, I needed confirmation that we were doing the right thing.

'Look, if you weren't grinding down that fertiliser, someone else would be doing it,' said Gerry. 'These bombs would get made and be set off with or without your help. Nobody's dying because of you. This is all about saving lives in the long term. The day will come when your information will prevent a really big one. You could single-handedly stop the next big IRA atrocity. You could stop the next Enniskillen.'

Alan joined in. 'We won't make you do anything you don't want to, Kevin. If it gets too heavy, we'll pull you out.'

'If you only ever save one life,' said Gerry, 'then your work will have been worthwhile.'

This single belief had to sustain me. Nobody was going to be killed that wouldn't have been killed anyway. If I save a single life, then it will all have been worthwhile. The idea of preventing an Enniskillen was just the motivation I needed.

A notorious incident in March of that year steeled me even more to carry on. Even by Northern Ireland's standards, March 1988 was a black month. First, the SAS shot dead three unarmed IRA terrorists in Gibraltar. The burials of these three took place in Milltown cemetery in Belfast. During the ceremonials, a Loyalist named Michael Stone ran amok, launching a grenade and a gun attack on the mourners. Three men died, dozens more were injured. Amid the carnage, Stone was chased to a nearby motorway. The RUC arrived in time to save his life.

One of the three men killed by Stone at Milltown was IRA member Kevin Brady. His funeral took place just a few days later on a Saturday afternoon. Amid the highly charged atmosphere, a car containing two men approached the funeral procession at high speed. Television cameras captured the events that followed – events that caused revulsion all around the globe.

The car was forced to stop and a pack of mourners set about it like savages. They pulled the two occupants out and started punching them and kicking them. A British army helicopter, circling like a hawk over a kill, relayed every sickening blow. The pictures shook as if they could barely cope with the horror of what they were conveying. The mob looked wired and high. Dressed in their Sunday best, they set about the two wide-eyed young men with brutal efficiency. There was a chilling inevitability about what would follow. The two bloodied victims were dragged to a patch of waste ground. There, we later found out, they were shot dead. They were corporals Derek Wood and David Howes, plain-clothes British army soldiers. They were armed, but they had chosen not to open fire on the mob that would later lynch them.

Their gory fates brought home to me the kind of people I

was dealing with. In the darkest recesses of the night, I hovered over my own execution. I saw myself getting dragged to waste ground, not by a baying mob but by Conor and Niall and Hardbap, all laughing hysterically. A black bin-liner is wrapped around my head and a gunshot sounds. Next thing, what is left of me is thrown into the crusher of a refuse truck – discarded like a piece of trash. At least it was only a dream. I wondered how the families of Corporals Wood and Howes coped, seeing it happening to their sons on the telly.

The fate of the two corporals shook me, but it also gave me a renewed determination. These were the good guys – undercover soldiers protecting this IRA funeral from the fate that befell the funeral of the Gibraltar Three in Milltown. Yet again, young British soldiers had stood in the way of Northern Ireland's warring factions, and paid the ultimate price. At least, that's how I saw it. I decided it was my duty as a British soldier to do right by my two fallen colleagues. I would make a difference so that their deaths weren't in vain.

Steeled with a fresh sense of purpose, I told Conor I had ground enough fertiliser – it was time I learned his entire repertoire of bomb-making skills. Flattery got you everywhere with Conor. Schooling a star-struck student really appealed to his ego. What shocked me most was how easy it was to construct these devices, and how all the component parts could be bought on the high street. For my first lesson, Conor invited me to watch him construct a booby-trap car bomb.

The 'up and under' mercury tilt-switch booby trap

consisted of a Tupperware box, two magnets, a plastic tube, a mercury ball and a quarter of a kilo of Semtex. The mercury ball was sealed inside the plastic tube. In effect, the metal ball acted as a conductor which triggered the explosion. The Tupperware box containing the booby-trap device would be strapped under a car, or placed in the footwell of the driver seat. It took just the slightest movement to make the mercury ball roll from one end of the sealed tube to the other – thus sealing the fate of anyone inside the vehicle. Such a small and simple device could blow an average family car to pieces.

Conor wouldn't tell me where the booby-trap device he had built that day was going. I was left to draw my own conclusions the next day when a builder in Kilkeel was killed after a bomb exploded under his car. The man's crime had been to carry out construction work for the security forces.

There were two other devices favoured by Conor. The so-called gas-bottle bomb was almost self-explanatory. The bottom end of a domestic gas keg would be cut off with an angle grinder. Homemade explosive – such as ground-down fertiliser and nitrobenzene – would be packed into the gas bottle. The bottom would be stuck back on with an industrial sealant.

Perhaps the most devastating and notorious IRA device was the fertiliser bomb. Whereas Semtex bombs were directional and far easier to control, fertiliser bombs were difficult to get right. As such, they had a tendency to cause far greater devastation than originally intended. Coupled with that, fertiliser dust was highly sensitive – if it got damp or compacted, it wouldn't go off at all.

By becoming a bomb-maker, I believed it was only a matter of time before I would become party to a planned atrocity – which I could then prevent. However, to get to this stage, I first had to become a tried and trusted IRA bomb-maker. I had to show that I could tailor any device to suit any situation. A bomb-maker had to show that his bombs could be trusted to achieve the desired result. It was all about judgement and skill and control – miscalculations in the past had cost lives and done untold damage to the IRA's reputation.

I got my first chance towards the end of 1988. Like me, a man I am referring to as Johnny was a bomb-maker learning his trade. Johnny was given the chance to construct his first major device. For legal reasons, I can't reveal my role in this operation. It was a massive squib, a seventy-pound fertiliser bomb. The target: Newry customs post. A small red van had been hijacked for the operation. The bomb was placed in the back of the van, which, just before lunchtime one weekday, was driven right up to the automated gates of the customs post. The horn was tooted and, to the amazement of the van driver, the gates buzzed open. He drove into the main yard, parked up where the bomb would cause maximum damage, got out of the van and walked up to the security booth. When the security guard heard what he had to say, he hit a panic button that alerted staff to evacuate. I watched it all unfold from a back-up car just across the road. I picked up the van driver and we headed to a designated safe house.

Driving off, I was relieved to see the customs workers swiftly vacating the building. I prayed quietly that there would be no casualties.

We got about half a mile up the road when a ground-shaking boom ripped through the air. To my horror, I heard myself emitting a triumphant roar. I had spent weeks grinding away on that device, and hearing the resulting explosion I felt a surge of professional pride. It was a perverse buzz, an unsettling sensation. I hoped I wasn't becoming one of them.

Back at the safe house, I switched on the radio. With a knot like a fist in my stomach, I waited to learn if there had been any casualties. I ran all the usual justifications through my mind, just in case. We had given the warning. The panic button had been sounded. We saw the workers leaving. Everyone had a chance to get well away before the device went off. I realised that these would prove facile justifications in the event of an innocent person losing their life. When the news bulletin came on, the bombing of Newry customs post wasn't the lead story – that was a good sign. Finally, the newsreader got to it. The customs post had been obliterated. Nobody had been hurt – my luck had held out again. As for Johnny, he had passed a major test. I would watch him rise swiftly through the ranks of the Provisional IRA.

Next it was my turn to prove my worth as a bomb-maker. My target? The Dublin to Belfast railway line in Newry. The objective? Closing the line for a week, thus causing chaos to the largely Catholic local community that the station served – the largely Catholic local community upon which the IRA relied for support. It would be a shame if innocent people – bound to be Catholic – got in the way. Sometimes, the sheer perversity of the IRA's thinking left me breathless.

Blowing up the line wasn't sufficient – that could be fixed in a day. The plan was to blow up a junction box. That should close the line for a week. Late one night, I climbed a fence near the station and made my way up the line. I inspected the junction box as best I could. I realised that blowing it up would require – as we were wont to put it – a good wallop. I reckoned it would need another seventy-pounder. Trouble was, the junction box was just three yards from the station building. If I blew up the junction box properly, I couldn't see how the station could escape. That meant potentially putting innocent lives at risk.

I took comfort from the fact that the station was completely deserted. I willed it to be similarly deserted in a few weeks' time. As I turned off the flash lamp and climbed back over the fence, I couldn't help smiling at the irony. Had it really been eight years since I had last closed this stretch of rail line with an empty can of Castrol GTX and a Tupperware box? I had come a long way since then. Whether it was in the right direction, I wasn't so sure.

I built a seventy-pound fertiliser bomb for the task. It was gone midnight when I parked up a few hundred yards from Newry train station. I had placed the fertiliser bomb and a battery timer in a holdall. I lifted it gently over the fence, then climbed over myself. During operations, I felt strangely unconcerned about getting caught. If an army unit or an RUC unit suddenly materialised out of nowhere, I'd suffer a rough few hours but eventually they would discover who I really worked for. Knowing how leaky the agencies were, I realised that the truth about who I was working for wouldn't stay a secret. My handlers would have to pull me out and relocate me. Mentally, this was something I had prepared myself for. As I placed the holdall next to the junction box, I wondered where they would send me. I hoped it would be somewhere sunny.

I set the timer and walked away as quickly as I could without making a noise.

It was just after one in the morning when the teeth-shattering boom started my wife from her sleep. I hadn't bothered going to bed. I knew I wouldn't get a wink of sleep that night. I switched on the TV and waited. In the pit of my stomach, the familiar knot had re-formed. I consoled myself with the groundless presumption that nobody would be hanging around Newry train station at one o'clock on a weeknight.

Finally, at three o'clock, a familiar stern flourish of brass announced the news. The knot tightened. In the searing rush of adrenaline, I seemed to take in only the words that mattered. Massive bomb; Newry train station badly damaged; shut for days; there are no reported casualties. With that, I exhaled what seemed like every ounce of energy within me. I had played another round of Russian roulette and survived.

By the time the early-morning bulletin came on, I was only half-listening from the kitchen. The po-faced newsreader seemed to be doling out exactly the same report. Then it cut to a reporter. As I got to the sitting-room door, I noticed the reporter standing in front of a bunk bed. In his left hand, he was holding what appeared to be a blackened lump of metal. He was looking terribly serious.

'This lump of railway line from last night's explosion came through the roof of the house and landed on the top bunk of this bed. Had the couple's young daughter been sleeping in that bunk, she would almost certainly have been killed.'

My legs and hands rattled. The knot in my stomach wanted out. I ran to the bathroom and dry retched into the sink. I splashed water over my face. It felt hot. I rubbed my eyes and thought hard. That lump of rail travelled a quarter of a mile. A child could have been killed because of me. Because I fucked up the mix. What was I thinking? 'You fucking idiot!' I bellowed into my shaking hands. I had miscalculated. I had put the lives of complete innocents at risk. I looked up and I looked hard at myself in the mirror. This was my lucky escape.

'I am a British soldier,' I told my reflection. 'I am a British soldier. I'm doing this to save lives. I'm saving lives. I'm a British soldier and I'm saving lives.'

Many more times in my career as a double agent, I would feel the need to stand in front of a mirror, take a long hard look at myself and repeat this mantra.

I got into the car and headed to Conor's in Dundalk. There was work to be done.

'Fuck me, what did you put in that mix?' said Conor in a mock-accusatory tone.

Clearly, a child narrowly escaping death was a great laugh for him. I couldn't even look him in the eye. I walked past him into his sitting room and flopped on to the sofa. At that precise moment, I thought, Fuck it, I'm jacking this in.

'Ach, look, nobody's been hurt,' said Conor, 'you didn't plan for it to happen that way.'

'Jesus, though, Conor, a little kid, I mean ...'

Conor's mood turned. What I saw scared me. 'Maybe you're not cut out for this,' he said sharply, 'because I can tell you now, you'll have closer shaves than that.' He turned to leave the room. 'Either pull yourself together now or go home. We've work to do.'

We were halfway through building a bomb for another operation in Newry. The target this time was a garage owned by a Protestant in Shandon Park; the device, another monstrous fertiliser bomb. A few nights later, I lay awake again waiting for the explosion. It never came.

Two days later, the development team was debriefed about what went wrong. The bomb had been planted inside the garage as planned, and the timer set. The team got away and a warning was rung in to the owner. Then nothing. For some reason, it didn't blow. The garage owner called the police, who in turn called the army's bomb-disposal unit. An army technical officer (ATO) went in to defuse the device. To IRA bomb-makers, ATOs are their nemesis. According to Conor, this was really who we were at war against. ATOs defused our bombs and thereby wiped out months of hard work at a stroke. An ATO getting blown up was the best possible news Conor could hear.

Apparently, the ATO was inspecting the bomb when it suddenly went bang. The detonating chord had gone off.

However, it failed to detonate the bomb. The fertiliser dust must have been damp or compacted. By all accounts, the experience scared the ATO half to death.

'Fuck,' said Conor, 'what a shame. We could have blown the fucker to kingdom come.' For days, he seemed wracked with regret over this missed opportunity.

Conor decided it was time the IRA hit back at the ATOs. He formed a special development team to figure out the best way of doing this. The team comprised myself, Johnny and Dermot Finucane (Pat's brother), the Maze Prison escapee.

We knew that, when they were called in to defuse a device, each ATO shared the same modus operandi. First, he checked the box timer to see how much time remained before detonation. Clearly, if it was a matter of seconds, he needed to start running. However, if he had any more than thirty seconds, he knew he could prevent the bomb going off simply by placing a piece of rubber or wood – his finger if it came to it – between two terminals inside the box timer. This stopped the box timer ticking down, which in turn stopped the bomb from detonating – just like in the movies.

The simplicity with which an ATO could defuse a bomb prompted the development team to research new detonation systems with the specific aim of slaughtering ATOs. Using their collective barbaric cunning, they came up with a new double-switch system of detonation. Under this system, as soon as an ATO touched a box timer, a highly sensitive micro-switch would be triggered. Unbeknown to the ATO, the micro-switch would override the box timer and set a new time frame for detonation – a much shorter time frame. The

ATO would think he was well ahead of schedule when the device would blow up in his face. The double-switch detonation system effectively meant that the box timer was booby-trapped.

To me, this was a highly irresponsible development. Let's face it: when an ATO walked in to defuse a device, he believed he was going to defuse it, not set it off. The double-switch system would trick the ATO into walking into his own death. Worse than that, it would put innocent members of the public in unnecessary danger. What if the police hadn't managed to clear the area around the bomb by the time the ATO had been sent in?

I told my handlers about this heinous new development. They assured me that the bomb squad would be fully briefed about it. 'Good work,' said Gerry, and I finally felt like I had supplied some really significant information, information that would save one life, maybe more. I felt like I had finally done some good as a double agent. This feeling didn't last long.

The development team put the micro-switch device through its paces. By spring 1989, the general consensus was that it was ready. Ready for what, exactly, I didn't know. I wouldn't be finding out until after the event.

I was parked up near the jetty in Omeath one morning in April 1989, waiting to pick up a delivery from an IRA man, when I heard this almighty wallop. Across the stretch of water, I could see a plume of smoke rising above the town of Warrenpoint. I assumed that the RUC station had been blown up; I hoped that some unfortunate ATO hadn't been blown up with it. I soon learned it was worse than that. Much worse. There was one eventuality of the double-switch system which none of us had foreseen.

A few days later, the man who drove the bomb into Warrenpoint told me all about it. A Hiace van had been hijacked for the operation. A massive fertiliser bomb was placed in the rear of the van, to be detonated by a box timer. To prevent an ATO defusing the bomb, the decision had been made to detonate it using the double-switch system. He parked the van as close as he could to the RUC station. Wasting no time to get away from the scene, he left the keys in the ignition. Adjacent to the RUC station was a hardware store. A customer went into the hardware store and complained that a van was blocking his passage out of the store's yard. A young employee went out to investigate, saw the keys in the ignition and moved the van so that it wasn't blocking the exit to the yard. He reversed it closer to the store.

The movement of the van triggered the micro-switch.

Meanwhile, Hardbap had decided to ring the bomb warning into the Daisy Hill Hospital in Newry. 'You're a bit late,' snapped the woman at the other end of the line, 'they're bringing in the casualties now.'

Seconds after the van had been moved, the bomb went off.

One teenage girl who worked in the hardware store was killed. Several others were injured. Another great day for the Provisional IRA. The slaughter in Warrenpoint was shrugged off as 'just one of those things'. Conor dismissed the horrendous blunder with the cliché that there were always innocent victims in war.

I was invited to join the development team full time. I agreed. At least this way I could warn my handlers about all future developments. We dedicated our every waking hour to the methodology of causing maximum carnage and destruction. Like crazed boffins, we were constantly experimenting with different explosive mixes, different detonators and different devices. We figured out a way to detonate Semtex in cider bottles, or inside the frame of a bicycle. We dragged our contraptions into the mountains to test them, before returning to our makeshift lab painstakingly to tweak and modify and adjust. Our lives were dedicated to the pursuit of a sort of grotesque perfection. It became all-consuming.

I was watching TV one night when an advert came on boasting about the incredible absorbency of a particular brand of tampons. The next day, I bought a box of heavy-flow tampons and soaked them in lighter fluid. The manufacturers would have been proud as punch. Each tampon absorbed the contents of three tubes of lighter fluid and burned for nearly twenty minutes. Tampons became an unlikely ingredient in our incendiary devices, and helped burn down several buildings, including the new Sprucefield shopping centre in Belfast.

Of course, being seen constantly in the company of men like Conor, Hardbap and Johnny, I soon became a target of the security forces. To the RUC, Special Branch and my former comrades in the British army, I was an IRA man. I was the enemy. The RUC stopped and searched me repeatedly, sometimes eight or nine times in a single day. Three officers in particular seemed hell-bent on making my life a misery. 'You fucking murdering Provo bastard,' they would say. 'We're gonna get our friends in the UVF to stiff you.'

A dig in the ribs was commonplace. They would take the ice-cream van apart, breaking anything breakable and deliberately contaminating the ice cream. 'Some of your old friends from the Royal Irish Rangers are coming to town at the weekend. We've told them where to find you. They're gonna give you a right old hammering.'

When the RUC wasn't provoking me, Special Branch would have a go. They would stop me and order a full security check over the radio. They made sure it took the best part of an hour. If I was selling ice cream, they would order me to shut down and sit in their car for a chat. Special Branch officers constantly tried to recruit me as a tout. Tell us what you know and we'll leave you alone. It became impossible to function normally in Newry.

Sometimes, the verbal threats became very real. On nine separate occasions, I was battered by the RUC. Once I had ceased working as a double agent, I sought them out to tell them the truth. They congratulated me on playing the role so well, and admitted that on more than one occasion they discussed ways that they might get me killed. In a way, I didn't blame them. I was an IRA man out to kill them and their colleagues. If I was in their shoes, I would probably have done the same. How were they to know we were working for the same side? I still don't hold it against them.

It was just as well really, because my handlers said they couldn't stop it. 'We can't trust ordinary plod officers in the

RUC with information like this,' said Alan. 'It's better for you that they think of you as an IRA man.'

'If they left you alone, it would look a bit strange, wouldn't it?' Gerry pointed out. 'It's testament to the excellent job you're doing.'

I did feel that I was doing exceptionally well. That my stock was rising within the IRA was beyond dispute. But my burgeoning reputation as a solid, dependable and efficient volunteer came with a significant down side. Increasingly, I was being ordered to carry out more important tasks on behalf of the IRA. More important tasks were inevitably more dangerous for me personally. Worse still, these tasks were getting closer and closer to outright terrorist activity. I never really imagined myself doing such things on behalf of the British army. I was convinced that a very distinct line existed, a line that agents would be ordered not to cross under any circumstances. Throughout the years, I clung to the belief that, as soon as I was ordered by IRA chiefs to do something that might kill or injure an innocent person, I would be pulled out by my handlers. But when my handlers sat back and let me construct bombs which ended up planted in the middle of towns and cities, I knew that this line had already been crossed. I now clung to the belief that, as soon as the IRA put me in a position where I would directly have to injure or kill someone, I would be pulled out by my handlers. The main flaw in this contingency plan, I was about to discover, was that it didn't take into account the very real possibility of being 'bounced' into a murderous operation.

To be bounced is to be given an order that you must carry out straight away. 'There's a squib leaving for Belfast right now, can you scout it up?' Hardbap asked a volunteer one afternoon. The volunteer had to jump straight into his car and carry out this task. Scouting basically involved driving well ahead of the vehicle carrying the bomb to check for army roadblocks or anything suspicious. Clearly, it was impossible for me to call a halt to any deadly convoy. If I got bounced into scouting a vehicle, what was I supposed to do? Hop out of my car into a coin box, give my handlers a quick call and then carry on? They would rumble me. If I was lucky, I would be instantly shot; more likely, I'd be tortured for a few days and then found in a ditch.

What was I supposed to do if I got bounced into an execution or into planting a bomb? I needed clarification from my handlers. Alan and Gerry were crystal clear on the matter. 'If you're bounced and you think it's going to be a spectacular against any of the security forces, then you must risk everything to try and find a way to alert us. We'll pull you out and that will be that. If you're bounced into planting a bomb or setting a landmine, try to make sure it won't go off, or make sure it goes off much earlier or later than planned. If you're bounced into kneecapping someone, aim high into the thigh.'

Little did I know that, over the next few years, I would be faced with each one of these scenarios. I realised eventually that there is no line. In the Dirty War, anything goes.

Weeks later, I was asked by Conor to drive a couple of volunteers to a pub in Mayobridge, County Down. I knew something was going on – I had developed a sixth sense with these people. The way they walked, the way they talked, the way they were so aware of their surroundings, I could tell that a spectacular of some sort was imminent.

A day later, in November 1989, the IRA detonated a landmine in Mayobridge that killed three members of the Parachute Regiment. I looked into the mirror that night and repeated the mantra. 'I am a British soldier. I am a British soldier obeying orders ...'

CHAPTER SIX

B y 1990, I lived in constant dread of being 'bounced' into some sort of murderous terrorist attack. The call could come at any moment. The caller could order a murder or a punishment shooting or a bomb attack down the phone like a takeaway pizza. To illustrate how callously efficient this Dial-a-Death service could be, let me tell you about an incident in which I was allegedly involved

It is said that on Easter Sunday night, me and another IRA volunteer were summoned to an address by Conor.

'What's going on?' I asked.

'You have to go to this number at Iveagh Crescent,' said Conor. 'We want a man there kneecapped.'

'Who?' I asked.

'Eoin Morley,' said Conor, 'that's his girlfriend's address, but I have it on good authority that he's there right now.'

I had heard about Morley. Until recently, he'd been a formidable figure within the Provisional IRA. By all accounts, he'd shot and killed a member of the security forces. Recently, he'd defected from the Provisional IRA to a splinter group called the Irish People's Liberation Organisation (IPLO). He'd also fallen out with Conor.

Myself and the second volunteer, a seasoned dispenser of so-called punishment shootings, were each handed a weapon. I assumed I was back-up, muscle. After all, I'd never done anything like this before. I then examined the weapon Conor specified he wanted used for the job. It was a high-velocity rifle. I was surprised. I thought a pistol would have been much more appropriate for a kneecapping.

'Isn't this a bit too powerful?' I asked rhetorically.

'Ach, no,' said Conor, 'it'll make a nice neat wee hole, that.'

'But, if the bullet hits a bone, it'll travel right up his body,' I said. 'This will kill him!'

Conor dismissed the pair of us with a wave of his arm. The decision had been made.

Clearly, I couldn't pull out – to bottle it at that juncture would be to dash all my hard work at a stroke. I would have been written off. 'He's only fit to sell papers,' they would say. I would never be trusted or included in anything serious again, or, worst-case scenario, the IRA would kill me. How could I expect to save lives if I wasn't even involved in Grade One IRA activity? Obviously, I couldn't stop and call my handlers. What could they do for me in such a situation anyhow? I could comfort myself with the knowledge that

Morley himself was a terrorist killer, someone who'd shown no mercy in the past. If I had to harm somebody to save the lives of the innocent, then this would probably be the kind of person I would pick.

As the car pulls into Iveagh Crescent, my concern shifts to my own survival. Morley's dangerous. He might be armed. I find it easy to switch my focus solely to the gory task in hand. There's nothing like the prospect of death or serious injury to distract the conscience.

As the car pulls up, the gunmen slide down their balaclavas. I follow my partner round to the back of the house. Silently, the senior IRA man slides bins up against the back door. I immediately twig. This is to prevent Morley making an escape.

We creep round to the front door. If you can give a friendly knock, I give it. A young woman answers. The masked men push past her into the house. She screams, great piercing screams. 'Get the fuck out, get out, get out!'

I don't know if she's shouting at us, or at the man desperately shouldering the back door. Suddenly, the man abandons the back door and charges towards us. He makes a grab for my gun. We fight like fuck. As I struggle to stay on my feet, I realise three things very quickly. Firstly, if Morley gets a good grip of a gun, someone other than Morley will wind up getting shot, maybe killed. Secondly, if we don't finish this thing very soon, one way or another there'll be neighbours in to help him and then it could get very messy indeed. Thirdly, the police will be turning up in a matter of seconds.

Just then, two shots ring out. Silence. Broken only by Morley crumpling to the floor. The gunmen turn and flee.

The next morning, I found out that Morley was dead. He was 23. His girlfriend was a mother of three. I felt more anger than guilt. This was no punishment shooting. From what I was told, the high-velocity rifle was used for the attack because the target was wanted dead. It didn't matter who was sent to Iveagh Crescent, or who pulled the trigger, Eoin Morley was going to die.

Later that week, I heard some news that filled me with dread. Morley's relatives were complaining loudly about the murder, and they had a close family connection to a giant within the Provisionals – Martin McGuinness. McGuinness was head of the PIRA's Northern Command and enjoyed an unrivalled reputation for ruthless efficiency. He was said to be taciturn and cold. People didn't *know* McGuinness, they only had dealings with him. He kept a distance. However, there was one common observation about McGuinness and his curious sense of morality: he would be in church praying one minute, then toughing it the next. He was perversely moralistic. He frowned on boozing and philandering – he could justify killing, though.

McGuinness was trying to distance himself from some of the violence of Republican activities. In recent years, he had assumed the bearing of a politician. He had removed himself from the day-to-day workings of the Provisional IRA and aligned himself publicly with Sinn Fein, the IRA's political arm. Sinn Fein saw no future in the armed struggle. The party had realised for some time that the way to bring about self-determination for the people of Northern Ireland was through winning seats, rather than killing and maiming. In reality, though, McGuinness still kept his style of leadership, while maintaining that politics and Republican activity were two separate things. In the late eighties, senior Provos told me that, if it wasn't for McGuinness, the IRA's military campaign may have been scaled down, or even brought to a halt.

When I learned that an internal investigation was being launched into the death of Morley, an icy chill ran through me. This was just the kind of scrutiny I didn't need. If I got on the wrong side of the investigator, my days would surely be numbered. What if he had contacts within the military? What if the Provos had the equivalent of me working within British intelligence? If I came to the attention of someone like McGuinness, strenuous new checks could be ordered.

A meeting with the key people involved in Morley's execution was organised for that week. The word was that Martin wasn't at all happy about what had happened, and had vowed to the Morley family to get to the root of the matter. I cringed at this news – it sounded like a witch hunt.

Before then, I had a meeting with my handlers. When I told them how Morley had been killed, their response was straightforward. 'Nice one,' they said. 'Let's hope they carry on killing their own.'

I was expecting a more robust examination of the facts from the internal IRA inquiry.

The meeting was at a house in Dundalk. A room with a large table had been prepared. Around the table sat Patsy

O'Callaghan, a big-shot IRA man from South Armagh, Conor, the man who we know as Johnny, IRA men from Newry and me. I fidgeted. The wait for the man conducting the inquiry, a senior Republican figure, was excruciating.

When he finally bustled in, O'Callaghan rose to his feet. 'Sit where you are, Patsy,' he said in his gruff accent. 'Right, guys,' he said, his stagnant eyes surveying us in a slow pan, 'I'm here to do an investigation into the killing of Eoin Morley. The Morley family say the two men were drunk, or at least under the influence. Is that right?'

'Are you here to stick up for the family?' said Conor. You had to admire his brass neck.

The senior man continued to look impassively around. It was like he was looking above our heads. He seemed preoccupied, bored, like he really had more important things to be getting on with.

I coughed in preparation to speak. He didn't look at me. Clearly, he wasn't going to deign to set his eyes on a lowly volunteer.

'I don't drink or smoke,' I said matter-of-factly. It was true too. I was never much of a drinker, but I'd packed it in completely two years earlier, around the time the IRA work started getting more serious. It was hard enough to see the angles without being pissed or hungover. I didn't want anything affecting my judgement.

My accomplice piped up too: 'I don't drink either,' he said. And it was true.

'That's good enough for me,' said the senior figure, and he turned to Patsy O'Callaghan and started a low animated chat.

We all looked at each other quizzically and wondered what was going to happen next. Was that the internal inquiry?

'Right, I'm off,' he said, getting to his feet, 'got a very busy schedule.' He didn't say goodbye as he strode out of the door.

It was now Patsy's turn to speak. 'From now on, don't go on jobs like this with a rifle. And there's no need to turn up armed to the teeth like the cavalry. Go in with one handgun and one baton. If the man about to be punished puts up a fight, one good whack of the baton should do the trick. Break his collarbone and the fucker will be in no mood to fight you.'

With that, the meeting ended. Everyone went their separate ways to resume their lives of terror. I couldn't help but wonder what the Morley family would be told. It was the first time I had dealt with the IRA leadership. I thought I had a measure of just how heartless that leadership could be. I was wrong. They could be far, far worse, as I found out later that year.

On 24 October 1990, the Provisional IRA launched one of its most despicable and cowardly attacks. It is said that I played a key role in the attack, something which, for legal reasons, I deny.

I knew something big was imminent. Days earlier, I'd been instructed to buy waterproof trousers and a waterproof jacket – a classic signal. Waterproofs were the standard uniform for a major job as they ensured no forensic evidence was left at the crime scene. I was then issued with a Webley .38 gun. I braced myself for the call.

It came that Wednesday, mid-evening. I was summoned to a house on the Derrybeg Estate. When I arrived, I was told to get across the road right away, as the unit was going out on a job that very instant. Fuck, I thought to myself, as I hurried across the road, what have they got planned now?

Waiting for me inside the door of the house was a lowly volunteer called David. 'Come on,' said David and I followed him to his car. We hopped in and headed down Rathfriland Road. I asked David what was going on.

'Dunno,' said David, 'we've to hijack a car and drive it to a garage on the edge of town. A few of the boys are waiting for us there. Seems the fucker who owns the garage is selling petrol to the peelers.'

We pulled in at some playing fields about two miles outside Newry. David knocked off the headlights. It was a cold, clear night, the stars peering down at us like a million cats' eyes.

'What the fuck is going on?' I said to David. 'Have we been told nothing at all?'

'No, but Fergus is in on it,' said David. He was referring to the newly promoted OC in Newry.

'Who else?' I asked.

'Patrick' said David.

He didn't see me wearily lift my eyes to those stars. Patrick was a big-mouthed hooligan, the very type the IRA could do without but seemed to attract in droves.

'That's it. That's all we know?' I asked, trying desperately to detect anything solid.

'That's all I know, anyways,' said David, climbing out of the car. 'Come on, we'd best get on with it.'

On our way to the roadside, I picked up a plastic bin. By now, I knew the drill as far as hijacking a car went. We waited in the dark until a set of car headlights shimmered white in the distance. I held the bin lengthways against my chest and waited. The car was seventy yards away when I hurled the bin out on to the road. The car slowed down quickly. David stepped out, pointed his gun at the windscreen and made sure the car stopped fully.

The man offered no resistance. He scrambled out of the car, his hands outstretched pleadingly, repeating the mantra, 'No problem, fellas. No problem at all.' The driver had already planted his hands firmly on his head when David nodded towards the playing fields. Off he walked, not daring to turn around, David behind him with his gun pointed at his back, poised in case our man made a run for it. You had to keep an eye on the really compliant ones, the ones who gave you no lip. Their compliance normally meant they weren't panicking but were thinking straight. Plotting.

'Put him on the ground,' I called, 'face down.' The last thing I wanted was our man making a dash for it, young David in hot pursuit, firing bullets.

When they disappeared from view, I surveyed the star-pricked sky and helped myself to a good gulp of air. I'd a bad feeling about all this. I hated not knowing. If it was all hush hush, then it was bound to be something truly horrific.

I psyched myself up with a 'Right, get on with it'. I climbed into the car, spun it around and drove back to Newry, and to whatever fate awaited me there.

The garage forecourt is deserted when I knock off the headlights and roll in silently. It looks like a classic family-run business – two petrol pumps, a little shop and a car showroom fronting a good-sized home. After a few minutes, a van with an Irish number plate pulls up on the edge of the forecourt – hijacked, no doubt. I recognise a chap called Fergus in the passenger seat, Patrick driving and the outline of a third figure squatting in the back.

I walk over to the passenger window and ask Fergus what our orders are.

'We've to secure the house,' says Fergus, 'then take the man of the house with us for a drive.'

I nod at Philip in the back. I ignore Patrick. I know he is chomping at the bit, desperate for action. He'd like nothing better than to go charging into the house, booting through doors, shouting and scaring everyone to death.

'Let me handle all the talking,' I say to Fergus.

'Fine,' he says and I can feel Patrick's resentful glare.

Experience has taught me that keeping everyone calm is absolutely crucial to a smooth operation. The sight of masked men with guns is normally enough to make your average family compliant. There really is no need for all that bawling and gun-waving. When masked men start shouting and waving guns about, panic gets the better of people. If hostages panic, gunmen panic. When gunmen panic, people die.

'OK,' I whisper, as we creep up to the front door, 'everybody nice and calm.'

I give the doorknocker a good workout. The sharp metal cracks echo loudly across the forecourt. Finally, the door opens. I push past a startled teenage boy into a sitting room. Fergus comes in next. He takes the arm of the young man who answered the door and leads him inside.

A woman in her late fifties sits in an armchair, facing the TV but looking at me. On the couch, a teenage boy and girl look up sharply.

'Sit down,' I instruct the young lad who answered the door. 'Right, is this everyone?' I say brightly, as if I'm about to start dishing out prizes.

'There's my husband. He's upstairs in bed,' she gasps. 'He's not at all well.'

Patrick slips off upstairs to get him. It's best in these situations to keep everyone together in one place.

'Listen,' I say, 'just relax and stay calm. We've no beef with you people.' To illustrate the point, I slip the gun into my jacket pocket.

'We need your help,' I go on. 'We're from the Irish Republican Army. One of our men has been injured out on the road. We need a car to take him to hospital.'

'No problem,' they say in unison.

'Take these, take these,' says the young man on the sofa, flourishing a set of car keys our way.

Now the mother pipes up. 'I'll show you where the keys are to all the cars in the showroom, if you like. You can help yourselves.'

Next thing, a man appears at the bottom of the stairs in a dressing gown, Patrick behind him. The man looks in an awful state, hunched and gaunt and almost yellow.

'Where are you taking him?' says the mother, alarmed.

'Settle down,' I say. 'This gentleman's going to help us get a car out of the showroom, that's all.'

'Look, let one of us do it,' says the teenage girl, already on her feet.

I'm taken aback by her apparent fearlessness. The last thing I need now is a bolshie woman.

'Sit down,' says Fergus sharply.

'Look,' says the mother, 'my husband is dying of cancer. He really isn't well at all. He shouldn't be out of bed.'

I survey their faces to see if they're having me on. They aren't. I look at the man. He's panting and slightly delirious. He's seriously ill. There really is no two ways about it.

Jesus Christ, I hear myself muttering. Nobody had mentioned any of this.

'Come on,' says Fergus, nodding to the poor man.

'Where are you taking him?' the mother shrieks. 'He's dying, for Chrissakes!'

'We're just taking a car,' I say calmly. 'We're bringing him back, then one of us will stay with you for a few hours.'

They seem reassured by this. Fergus and I follow the old man out the front door. He's barely able to walk. As he feebly pads across the forecourt, I feel a lump in my throat. I try not to think about my own father in such a situation, a noble old man being ordered about by a bunch of young thugs.

I help the old man over to the hijacked car and into the back seat. Before I can stop him, Patrick has slid in alongside him. He insists on blindfolding the poor old devil, and presses a gun into his ribs. I feel a surge of fury. I desperately want to admonish Patrick – 'For fuck's sake, what can this poor bastard do to us?' – but I hold my tongue. It will have to wait for later.

I drive back to the playing fields in the hijacked car, Patrick and the old man in the back, Fergus behind us in the van. As I wheel into the playing fields, the headlights pick out David standing over the driver of the hijacked car, who's prostrate on the ground. I feel strangely gratified to see that David has taken my advice. If I could contribute nothing else positive to this dreadful operation, at least I'm eliminating fuck-ups that could lead to needless injury or death. Fergus joins us in the car. It's now David's job to take the driver of the hijacked car back to the house where the dying man's family is being held. It's always a good idea to keep all your hostages together in one place.

Fergus tells me to drive to the town of Omeath across the border. As the old man wheezes and groans in the back, we drive on in silence. We feel embarrassed. Besides, it might sound selfish, but I'm busy wondering what the hell we do in the event of the old fellow keeling over on us there and then. Now that would be a problem.

Fergus directs me around the streets of Omeath until we pull up outside a bungalow. 'Hang on here,' he says, and strides inside purposefully. Seconds later, he emerges with someone called Johnny, a bomb-making graduate.

'Follow us,' says Johnny, and we do, along the winding back roads around Carlingford Bay, through black trees, water glistening silver under bright moonlight. The beauty seems inappropriate, an ill-judged accessory to whatever horrific end awaits this sorry figure crumpled in the back seat, wheezing and groaning.

Johnny and Fergus turn left into a well-known beauty spot. I follow. The roads around here are a favoured spot for dumping bodies. Christ, I think to myself, they're going to shoot him.

I pull up. 'Right, get him out of the car,' comes the barked order.

The old fellow gingerly crawls out and staggers about, still blindfolded.

'Walk this way,' comes a voice, and off he sets on unsteady feet.

I follow the old man into the amenity area. Waiting for him, dramatically silhouetted against the moonlight, stand ten men with guns. Christ, I think, this is a bit over-the-top.

The armed men have their hoods pulled up, so Patrick and myself follow suit. After a lot of hushed chatter, Fergus comes over to us. 'We've to go back to Derrybeg,' he says.

I don't need to be told twice. I don't care to witness whatever grotesque pageant is about to be played out here. I can't bear to watch his emaciated frame stumbling about for another second.

Once back on the road, I turn to Fergus in the passenger seat. 'What the fuck is going on?'

'I can't really say,' says Fergus, trying not to look like he hasn't the faintest idea.

'Could we not have just blown up his garage?' I say.
Silence.
We get back to the house in Derrybeg for midnight. The

rule is we all stay together until told otherwise. This is to ensure that any mole amongst us wouldn't have the chance to sneak off and alert the security forces. There's nothing anyone can do but wait. The night drags. We don't talk about the old man any more.

At about five in the morning, an almighty bang nearly lifts the roof off the house. Even Fergus looks stunned. We try to figure out how this bomb might be connected to our handiwork the night before. It just doesn't make sense. In the end, we assume that the bombing's a separate attack, probably on the tax office. Then the call comes through. We can all go home. The two incidents must have been connected, but how?

I found out next morning. Over the following two days, the full extent of this heinous IRA operation was revealed. The man I had helped to abduct was one of three Catholic civilians forcibly taken from their homes by the IRA that night. In each case, the man was forced into the driver's seat of a van loaded with one tonne of explosives and given instructions to drive towards British army targets. The captives had been turned into the IRA's latest and most contemptible weapon: human bombs. The three men, strangers to one another, had in common only the fact that they were regarded as collaborators by the IRA because of their employment or business dealings with the security forces.

The three vans were closely followed by cars filled with IRA gunmen. They served as tails to ensure that their unwilling drivers followed their instructions. As well as carrying guns, each tail car carried a remote-control detonator to set off the explosives. As an extra precaution, the doors to the vans had been booby-trapped. If a driver tried to make a run for it, he would go up with his load.

The first human bomb was forty-two-year-old Patsy Gillespie from Derry. The target was a British army/RUC checkpoint on the outskirts of the city. Patsy Gillespie got there at about a quarter past four. As he slowed to stop, the IRA escort peeled off and sped away. At that moment, the van blew up. The explosion was powerful enough to flatten the checkpoint's concrete-block fortification and severely damage twenty nearby homes. Five British soldiers were killed, five more injured. Patsy Gillespie died instantly. He was a father of four and a cook for the British army.

The second human bomb was the man I had helped to abduct. Colman McAvoy was sixty-five and a father of six who occasionally serviced vehicles for the RUC. He drove the van to a checkpoint in Killeen, just outside Newry, on the main Dublin to Belfast road. This is the border's busiest checkpoint. Most traffic going to or from the Irish Republic comes through it. At five in the morning, it was deserted except for soldiers and RUC officers. However, the IRA men tailing McAvoy were in for a surprise.

Johnny was a ruthless IRA operative who would think nothing of planting a bomb that might kill civilians, or of shooting a policeman, a British soldier or an informant in cold blood. Even Johnny couldn't stand the sight of this sick old man, wheezing and spluttering, driving to a certain death. Johnny told him to pull up at the checkpoint, unwind the window and exit the van that way. 'Run like fuck and do not look back,' he told me was his specific instruction.

McAvoy drove to the checkpoint as instructed, unwound the window and scrabbled out. A British soldier told him to move his van but, having escaped certain death once, McAvoy wasn't keen to go back. 'There's a bomb in the van,' he shouted, over and over.

'Get back and move the van,' the soldier shouted.

When McAvoy refused to budge, the soldier grabbed him and started dragging him back to the van. God only knows what must have been going through McAvoy's mind. The explosives went off, killing the British soldier and injuring fourteen of his colleagues. Human bomb McAvoy suffered a broken leg.

The third human bomb was forty-two-year-old Gerry Kelly, who lived with his wife and child in Omagh town. He was abducted from his home by masked men, strapped into a van full of explosive and ordered to get as close as possible to the British army barracks in Omagh. Gerry did what he was told. 'The sweat was dribbling down my face. All sorts of things were going through my mind. I thought this was it,' he told a newspaper after the event.

Kelly survived because the explosives failed to go off. He had been targeted because he worked as a mechanic at a local British army facility.

In all, seven people died and thirty-six people were injured as a result of that night's human-bomb attacks. Even the battle-scarred people of Northern Ireland were shocked.

I felt disgusted that we'd failed to stop these 'human

bombs' attacks. I had to balance the death of that soldier by saving more lives. I wanted to use my position in the Provisional IRA actively to prevent someone from being murdered. If I could save more lives than I helped to take, then my role as a special agent would be worthwhile and justifiable. It might sound simplistic, but this was the only way I could logically navigate my way through the madness of this Dirty War. Of course, I never lost sight of the risks to myself. I knew that to compromise my own position within the IRA was to bring about certain death. Despite that, I felt a moral duty to take more risks.

After all, if it all went wrong, I knew my handlers would pull me out.

Thanks to my meteoric ascent within the IRA, opportunities to save lives and ensnare leading IRA people soon started to present themselves. I grasped them with relish. We owed it to Colman McAvoy, and to my fellow British soldier who'd been slaughtered at Killeen.

The outcry that greeted the human-bomb campaign did little to sate the IRA's appetite for slaughtering so-called legitimate civilian targets. Anyone working for or supplying a service to the security services in any capacity was seen as fair game. In twisted IRA logic, Catholic building labourers and Catholic milkmen and Catholic toilet cleaners now obstructed their pre-destined, God-given right to a United Ireland.

And so one IRA unit's next mission was to try to shoot building workers reconstructing the Ardmore police station on the Armagh Road in Newry. A team of four had been hand picked for the task. It is said that they were led by me.

I was to be in charge of two more gunmen and a driver. The IRA meant business: a GPMG and two AK-47s were produced for the job.

The OC outlined the plan. The night before the attack, we would take over a house near the RUC station. We would research which house to take in advance. However, it would need to have two cars sitting in the drive, as we needed two for the operation.

'Try to aim for the home of an SDLP supporter,' said the OC, 'as we put our own off when we steal their cars for operations.'

From an IRA point of view, targeting SDLP supporters over those of Sinn Fein, the IRA's party, held other key advantages. The SDLP (Social Democratic Labour Party) is the more moderate Catholic party, supported by educated middle-class Catholics. As such, SDLP people tended to live in large, private detached homes that offered more seclusion for the impromptu terrorist visit. And they were more likely to own two cars.

The getaway driver would bring the first car to a secret spot where we would rendezvous after the attack. The following morning, the other two gunmen and I would drive the second family car to a building site directly across the road from the RUC station. We would use disguises to get into this building site – again, we'd have to use our own initiative – but, once inside, the half-built homes would provide perfect cover for a gun attack. After mowing down as many building workers as possible, we would make our getaway. We would drive to a certain street where we would meet the driver of the second stolen car. He would drive us to an agreed safe house. We would lie low there for a few hours, then head home, making sure we had copper-bottom alibis worked out in advance.

After some research, we selected our host family. The man of the house was deceased; his widow shared the home with two grown-up children. That evening, we tiptoed past two glistening saloon cars to the front door.

When confronted by masked men, ordinary people get such a shock that they tend to put up no resistance whatsoever. Most don't even check to see if you're armed. While my sidekicks bound and gagged the quivering trio, I calmly assured them that they would come to no harm.

I cut the telephone wires and we took it in turns to watch them throughout the night. There are strict rules when taking over a home for an op. If someone rings the doorbell – be it a pizza delivery boy or a family friend or a Jehovah Witness or Gerry Adams – you must take them in and tie them up too. Another golden rule is to avoid leaving any forensic traces. You don't drink out of any of the cups. You keep your gloves and hat on at all times. You don't use the loo.

As nine o'clock approached the following morning, that old familiar knot took a firm grip on my stomach. I was treble-checking my machine gun when excited calls came from upstairs. I ran up to the front bedroom to find my two cohorts aiming their AK-47s out of the window.

'What the fuck ...?' I spluttered.

'Look,' said gunman one, cocking his gun, 'it's like fucking Christmas!'

A five-strong British army foot patrol was less than a hundred yards from the house.

'Come on,' he said, training his AK-47 on the soldiers and licking his lips, 'it'll be like shooting fish in a barrel.'

Christ, I thought, how the fuck do I talk them out of this? 'No,' I heard myself saying, 'we don't know what's behind them.'

'What?' said the gunmen together.

'Look at them,' said gunman one, still following the patrol with his weapon, his finger twitching on the trigger, 'we can pick 'em off from here no bother, then get out through the back garden. Come on, it's a gift!'

'Look,' I said, 'the RUC station is two minutes up the road. We've no getaway planned. The safe house isn't expecting us yet. Our getaway driver is parked up on a street somewhere.'

'Come on,' said gunman two, 'let's do it.'

My mind was racing, boggling at this dilemma. There was no way I was going to let these two scumbags mow down five British soldiers. If they opened fire now, what would I do? I couldn't shoot a British soldier. I would deliberately have to miss. What if the soldiers started firing back? Did I want to get into a gunfight with people on my own side?

As my comrades for the day observed the soldiers, I observed them. Slowly, I raised my machine gun up to chest height. I wasn't going to stand back and watch these men kill five of my colleagues. If it came to it, I'd pull my weapon on them. To hell with the consequences.

'No,' I said firmly, 'we're following strict orders. We must stick to the original plan.'

'Forget the fucking builders,' shouted gunman one, 'we've got soldiers here in our sights!'

'No,' I said. 'I'm in charge and I say no. That's an order.'

I had a firm grip on my gun, my finger fixed ready. They could have had no idea what was going through my mind when, reluctantly, they lowered their weapons. I wondered if they could hear my heart pounding. I wondered if this would get back to the OC. What would I say? What possible justification could I give for not availing myself of this golden opportunity to pick off a British army patrol? With the weapons at our disposal at that moment, we could have mown them down in seconds. No doubt someone like Conor would have taken their chances and gone for the soldiers. I thought I better have a damn good excuse ready.

The spared foot patrol passed the house, oblivious to their narrow escape. We were headed to a building site and wanted to blend in. We also wanted to ensure we couldn't be identified, and that we would leave no forensic evidence. A few days earlier, the white boiler suits seemed a good idea. So did the monkey hats and the fake moustaches. However, as we climbed into the family saloon, I caught a glimpse of us in the side window. We didn't look like a crack IRA unit on a dangerous mission. We looked like a GameBoy Mario tribute act.

When we got to the building site across the road from the RUC station, a group of idlers in hard hats stood smoking out the front. 'We're not ready for the painters yet,' said one, as we marched into the site.

Inside, four labourers nailing plasterboard ceilings looked down at us. 'What the fuck are you doing?' one of them guffawed.

We produced our weapons and they stopped guffawing. Suddenly, the sound of tools dropping echoed across the site. It was about half past nine when we stood at an unglazed upstairs window, surveying the target some 600 yards away. A couple of days earlier, bricklayers in bulletproof vests could be clearly seen working outside the station.

'Fuck,' I said, 'where are the builders?'

We waited and waited. Of course, I knew there would be no builders working on the RUC station today. I had tipped off my handlers about the plan.

'They're probably inside,' said one of the team. 'What the fuck will we do now?'

'We'll shoot them inside,' I said, raising the machine gun, 'that's what we'll do now.'

My handlers had assured me that the building site would be cleared for the day. I now had the chance to look dangerous, to impress my underlings so they would go back to IRA chiefs saying what a bold, brave, crazy, reckless motherfucker Kevin Fulton was. After my failure to portray myself in this way once today, I wasn't going to let this opportunity slip.

I started firing round after round at the building. To be absolutely safe, I aimed at the walls and over the building. The other two joined in.

'Shit, what was that,' said one of them and we stopped. Concrete snapped off in lumps behind us.

'The fuckers are firing back!' said the other one, pointing at bullet holes in the walls.

I couldn't believe it. My people had tipped off the RUC and what thanks did I get? Being shot at, that's what. I was furious. I had taken a huge personal risk saving these people from attack. Now here they were trying to kill me.

'Right, fuck 'em,' I said out loud, and we laid into the building for a full five minutes. I must have fired off 200 rounds without ceasing.

When we came out of that building site, the streets were deserted. Suddenly, I heard the sound of cheering. We looked down the road and there, at the windows of the school next to the building site, stood hundreds of kids clapping and whooping at our escapade. We had to laugh.

We drove to the back end of a council estate, jumped out and put our boiler suits, hats, fake moustaches and balaclavas in a heap on wasteland. Just then a girl I knew walked by. She decided not to look. A Lucozade bottle full of petrol was produced from the boot and the props set ablaze. We hopped back into the car and took a pre-planned back route to another estate. Here our driver was waiting in the second car. As sirens pierced the morning air, we abandoned the first car on waste ground, set it alight and jumped into the second car. Off we sped to another estate where we abandoned the second car and ducked into a safe house.

Here we formed an orderly queue to shower and change

clothes. As soon as we had got rid of all traces of the operation, we were free to go. Nobody could prove a thing.

The next day, I found out that a round from a sub-machine gun had buckled a piano in a family home on the other side of the RUC station. Thankfully, the house had been empty at the time. Of course, the IRA boys thought this was hilarious and I had to play along. I certainly couldn't admit that I had deliberately aimed high to avoid hitting anyone around the station.

Away from IRA eyes, I was furious with myself. I had neglected to check out the other side of the RUC station in advance of the attack. I'd been careless. As a result, I had peppered a family home with machine-gun fire. I could have wiped out an entire family. I had come that close to killing an innocent person. What the hell was I thinking? I felt fate closing in on me. How many more times would I be that lucky?

CHAPTER SEVEN

On the morning of 7 February 1991, the British war cabinet met at the very epicentre of British political power: Number 10 Downing Street. Led by John Major, the cabinet had convened for urgent discussions about the ongoing Gulf War.

Just after ten o'clock that morning, the windows shattered. Politicians and civil servants dived for cover. A mortar bomb had landed in the garden of Number 10. It had been launched from a firing position at the corner of Horseguards Avenue and Whitehall, hitting a tree and landing fifteen yards short of its target. Two more mortars quickly followed. Both overshot their target, causing damage to numbers 11 and 12.

The attacks made headlines around the world. Britain was at war and in the throes of a well-publicised security clampdown, yet the IRA had managed to get within fifteen yards of the war cabinet.

I was able to tell my handlers who was behind the attack on Downing Street.

After all, it was well known amongst Provos that one man controlled all IRA terrorism activity in England and on the continent. For legal reasons, I cannot name him in this book; I shall refer to him as Stephen.

Stephen and Conor went back a long way. Long before the Downing Street attack, I had told my handlers everything I had found out about Stephen from my IRA mentor. Quite what they did with this information I never knew.

I explained how he sat on the all-powerful, five-strong IRA Army Council. The Army Council ran the Provisional IRA. Every decision – from overall strategy right down to whether or not a volunteer-turned-informant should live or die – came down to the vote of the Army Council.

This man held a seat on the Army Council because he ran the South Armagh brigade of the IRA – the most terrifyingly efficient and close-knit unit in the organisation. If the South Armagh brigade recruited volunteers from another unit for an operation – such as it did for the human-bomb campaign – those volunteers wouldn't be privy to the details of that operation until the final seconds. It was Stephen and his men who helped South Armagh gain its reputation as bandit country.

Most crucially, I was able to reveal to my handlers that this man was the sole supplier of mortar bombs to the IRA. Building and launching mortars required a certain expertise. He and his team were the acknowledged experts. I knew this because I had heard Conor order three from him for a job in Newry.

At the time, the Newry courthouse was being renovated. Anyone working on the building – that is, working for the security forces – was considered a legitimate target. The IRA dealt in terror, and slaughtering lowly workers going about their daily routine spread terror more efficiently than any other tactic. Ordinary workers held another attraction for these cold-blooded opportunists. Unlike soldiers, policemen and politicians, workers were not armed or protected. As such, they were easy meat. So the builders renovating Newry courthouse became Conor's next target.

To protect workers from potential attack, a massive blast wall had been constructed around the entire courthouse structure. A blast wall consisted of two breezeblock walls erected one behind the other, about four feet apart. The gap between the walls was packed with sand. The typical blast wall can withstand bombs, grenades, charging vehicles and gunfire.

However, the one thing a blast wall can't repel is a mortar bomb. I knew that mortars, if launched properly, could be propelled over the blast wall directly into the building site. The impenetrable blast wall would then act as a compression chamber, trapping the devastating power of the mortars inside its structure and creating a pinball machine of burning shrapnel. Nobody inside that blast wall would survive the rebounding aftershocks. Each day, about 100 workers toiled within the supposed safety of those blast walls.

Conor was forthcoming about everything but the actual date of the attack. He told me that three massive mortar bombs known as barrack-busters had been commissioned for the attack. Barrack-busters were industrial gas cylinders weighing eighty or ninety pounds and packed with explosives. The mortars would be launched from a van parked in a car park across the road from the courthouse. The roof of the van would be cut out and replaced with paper sprayed the same colour. I had seen it done before. From a foot away, you couldn't tell the difference. At least not until the mortars had ripped through it.

Launched like rockets, mortars are uniquely difficult to control and aim. They are self-propelled. To hit the courthouse, they would have to get over the blast wall but not overshoot. The trajectory and distance would have to be worked out precisely beforehand. An inch in the car park translated as several feet across the road.

Using a Trumeter distance-measuring wheel favoured by ordnance workers, the team had already calculated the exact spot in the car park from which the mortars would be launched. Conor was confident they would hit the target. The men tasked with driving the van to the car park and launching the mortars had already been on a detailed dummy run. Experienced in the delicate art of aiming mortars, the driver had apparently placed white marks on the windscreen that tallied with fixed points on the courthouse. On the day of the attack, he could use these marks as reference points to ensure that he had got the position of the launch van absolutely right.

I knew that the attack was imminent, but I wasn't able to give my handlers any idea as to exactly when it would happen. It could have been days, weeks or months. In terms of preventing the mortar attack, their options were surprisingly limited. The army could stake out the car park, but for how long? It couldn't remain there indefinitely. That wasn't the only judgement call that needed to be made. How many people would turn up as part of the bombing team? Would they be armed? To ensure the safety of the soldiers – and to prevent the embarrassment of being overpowered – the army would have to deploy a significant number of personnel. How could they do this covertly? No doubt, IRA spotters were already keeping a close eye on the car park.

Besides, if the IRA unit was ambushed at the scene, I would be left badly exposed. Only Conor and the famously tight-lipped volunteers from South Armagh were privy to the exact details of the attack. In such a reputable chain, Conor would no doubt finger me as the weak link.

While military intelligence pondered the dilemma, the RUC erected roadblocks on all routes leading to the courthouse. Of course, they couldn't do this indefinitely, but it protected the workers for now and, crucially, bought some time. However, we knew that, once the roadblocks were gone, the courthouse was vulnerable. There had to be some other way of preventing the attack.

Desperate to thwart the bombers, my handlers sent a scout down to examine the car park. It was an inspired decision. That very evening, a height-restriction barrier was erected at the car-park entrance, preventing entry to all vehicles save cars and motorbikes. Clearly, IRA spotters hadn't noticed the new height restriction. The next morning, the van carrying the mortars turned up at the car park.

It couldn't get in.

Instead of turning away, the IRA unit drove to an industrial estate on the outskirts of Newry. From there, it fired the mortars at what was obviously a regular target – a poorly protected UDR station. However, having not worked out the trigonometry in advance, the mortars bounced harmlessly into a field. The attack had been thwarted without a single loss of life. Better still, the failure of the attack couldn't be linked to me in any way. The sudden appearance of the height-restriction barrier was dismissed by Conor as 'one of those things'. It was the worst kind of luck – nothing more.

When I next met the handlers, we celebrated hard. This was a real result. We had saved lives for sure, maybe more than 100. In all my time as a double agent, this was a rare but glorious high point. Finally, all the years of lying and worrying and being party to terrorism seemed worthwhile.

The elation never lasted long, though. The victories inevitably felt hollow, because I couldn't share the joy with the person in the world who mattered most to me: my wife. I couldn't bore her with the setbacks either. To her, I was an IRA man and so the work I did was not part of our everyday lives. She asked no questions about anything that happened to me from the time I walked out the front door until the moment I got back. It might sound shocking, but this was a war situation and this was how marriages survived the carnage. When my wife married me, she thought she knew what I was involved in and she accepted the inevitable secrecy and loneliness. IRA wives know better than to implicate themselves in any way. Their commitment to ignorance about what their husbands are up to is what keeps most IRA families together.

This wasn't the first time I had saved lives, nor would it be the last. Worryingly, though, I knew that the chance of me contributing to the death of innocent people was as present as ever. I was still working for the IRA's bomb-development team. By the early 1990s, we were immersed in a technical battle with the British army's bomb-disposal experts – a battle they were winning. They had made radio-controlled bombs a thing of the past. For a start, they were continually improving the protective radio-wave shields they had now flung around every police station, army base and military vehicle. This shield blocked signals between radio-controlled devices – no matter how sophisticated – anywhere in the vicinity. Bombs simply couldn't be detonated anywhere close by.

Once an IRA radio bomb had failed to detonate, the army could retrieve the weapon and identify the radio code on the receiver, thus neutralising all bombs using the same signal. When this occurred, the IRA could spend months trying to find a new signal that would break through the shield.

To add to our woes, patrolling soldiers carried radio-wave disruptor packs on their backs, spoiling everyone's TV reception and jamming up the IRA's radio-signal communications. The army had also developed a scanner capable of detecting radio emissions instantly, thus pinpointing devices and the personnel planning to press the button. In short, we needed to work out a way of detonating a bomb from a distance that didn't involve using a radio signal.

I can't remember who came up with the idea first, but one of the team knew a stills photographer. That photographer explained how, instead of erecting lights for some studio shoots, he set up a system of slave-unit flashguns which simultaneously triggered each other off. Once you fired one flashgun, it then triggered off all the others.

This got the team thinking. We quickly worked out that, by attaching a flashgun slave unit to a detonating system, detonation could be triggered by simply aiming a flashgun at the slave unit and flashing it once. After days of fevered experimentation, we realised that a bomb could be detonated this way from a distance of 100 metres. To detonate the bomb, all that was required was a bog-standard flashgun and a slave unit that could be bought over the counter in any photographic shop on the high street. The flashgun system of detonation was simple, cheap, effective and impossible to jam. In short, without a state-of-the-art lab, a huge budget or any academic credentials between us, we cracked it.

The more we experimented with the flashgun device, the more we realised its devastating potential. On learning that a local milkman was delivering produce to the RUC station in Newry, the local IRA came up with a breathtakingly ruthless plan to announce the new flashgun detonation system to the world.

The plan was simple. Early one morning, an IRA unit would go to a house on the Armagh Road to which the milkman delivered milk daily. The owner of the home – a middle-aged woman who lived on her own – would be taken away and held at a safe house. The rest of the unit would wait for the milkman to call. When he did, he would be dragged into the garage of the house and executed. His body would then be laid out on the hall floor. Next came the really clever part.

The milk inside six cartons would be emptied out and replaced by Semtex and a flashgun slave unit. The six cartons would be resealed and left beside the milkman's dead body in the hallway. The IRA unit would then leave.

Eventually, someone would call at the house and see the body, or a neighbour would ring the RUC on account of the fact that a milk float had been sitting outside the house for several hours. The RUC officers would walk in through the front door and find the body. They would call for back-up and for a forensics team. A scene-of-crime officer would arrive to take photographs. As soon as his camera flash went off, the whole house and everyone inside it would go up.

I warned my handlers about the plan and left it to them to do something about it. I learned some days later that the milkman suddenly announced his retirement. I had saved his life, but I knew that Conor and the team were still desperate to christen the flashgun device. My new handlers were equally desperate to be briefed about it so that they could somehow combat its simple genius.

By now, the latter part of 1991, I had two new handlers – one from the Force Research Unit (FRU) and, for the first time, a handler from MI5. Clearly, the information I was now supplying had been judged of national importance. Officers from RUC Special Branch were invited to sit in on our meetings in case anything of direct relevance to them came up. However, the men who planned my every move were Pete from FRU and Bob from MI5. They did things very differently. There were no more meetings in lay-bys or games of pool or trips to a shooting range. I met Bob two or three times a week, every week. I travelled all over Northern Ireland for our rendezvous – always well away from Newry. We had four favoured places to meet – in Dromore, Hillsborough, Newtonards and Dundonald Hospital. To thwart anybody bugging our calls, we coined these locations spots one, two, three and four. The beauty of mobile-phone technology was that we could select any of these locations for our meeting at very short notice. To further guarantee my personal security, I was armed with a pager.

On arriving at one of our locations, I would be helped into the side door of a blacked-out van and whisked off to a secret location – not for a chat but to be debriefed. This was truly the stuff of a John Le Carré novel.

The places I was brought to all had integral garages with doors leading directly into the building. I would be led along the hallway of a very expensive home towards a dining room or a sitting room. I remember one of these homes sporting expensively framed caricatures of leading British politicians all the way up the hall. The house's owner – who never showed his face – used to whip up the most spectacular curry dishes for us to eat while we got on with our business. In my head, I had an image of the man as a sort of red-faced, brandy-swilling major who listened to BBC Radio 4 and spoke endlessly about his military service in India.

Occasionally, when there was something of particular

significance to discuss, Bob from MI5 would call me on the mobile phone and tell me an airline ticket to London was waiting for me at Aldergrove Airport. In late March 1992, I was put up in a flashy central London hotel for one such visit, having informed my handlers that Conor was planning an attack using a flashgun and doodlebug. For two days, I was debriefed by military intelligence, the Home Office, the Anti-terrorist Branch, RUC Special Branch and MI5 about the new flashgun device that I had helped to develop. They seemed, by turns, horrified and deeply impressed by its barbaric simplicity. Little did I know that as we spoke in the boardroom of a posh London hotel – the room had been booked under a false business name – the flashgun device was being dusted down for a horrific attack.

I got back on Friday, 27 March. In a grim twist of fate, the flashgun device was used in spectacular fashion that very night. While I was briefing the British security forces, it was being used to attack two of their employees.

A large hole had been sawn out of the side of a car boot – the rear right-hand side to be exact – with an angle grinder. The hole was disguised by paper sprayed the same colour as the car. In the boot, facing that hole, lay a primed horizontal mortar, also known as a Mark 12 rocket. Shaped like a missile, the mortar had a copper coned warhead stuffed with a kilo of Semtex.

On the windscreen of this car sat a photoflash slave unit and a trigger mechanism. A wire ran from this slave unit through the dashboard and out through the back seat of the car, all the way to the mortar in the boot.

The car was parked on Merchant's Quay in Newry, alongside the canal. One hundred yards away stood an IRA man with a flashgun. He spotted an unmarked police car driving along the quay. As the police car drew alongside the booby-trapped car, he flashed the flashgun at the windscreen. An electrical circuit was created, triggering a detonator which then set off the missile. The police car was only a few feet away when the missile slammed into its side. The bang shook the glass out of every window on the street. The car careered into a line of parked cars. It took ambulance men and the fire brigade fifteen minutes to cut out the two officers inside. Surgeons fought for several hours to save the life of Constable Colleen McMurray. They failed. She was thirty-four and recently married. Doctors pumped sixty-six pints of blood into her colleague, Constable Paul Slaine. It was pouring out as fast as they were pumping it in. He survived, but lost both legs. His throat was slashed. He was a twenty-eight-year-old father of three.

When I called down to a bar in Dundalk two nights after the attack to see Conor, they were still joking about it. More than once, a drunken IRA man came up behind Conor, tapped him on the shoulder, waited for Conor to turn and then pretended to take his photograph. 'Say cheese, motherfucker!' he roared to howls of hilarity. Conor joined in and it became clear that everyone in this bar room believed that he had been the man who had activated the flashgun on Merchant's Quay.

These days, I feel terrible about the death of Constable McMurray and the injuries suffered by Constable Slaine. To be honest, though, back in 1992 I felt very little. In my full-time role as a double agent, I was losing any sense of myself. When I was with my comrades in the Provisional IRA, I morphed into a character I no longer felt any emotional attachment to. I was so in character that I stopped feeling the pain and the doubts and the anguish – all those emotions which would hinder my efficiency as a double agent. I was becoming de-sensitised, de-humanised, robotic. This seemed to suit everyone. Especially me.

That said, there was no danger of me 'turning'. I still knew which side I was on and, before 1992 was out, I would tilt the balance back in our favour. Firstly, I saved another life.

For the first time ever in my IRA career, I was ordered to kill someone in cold blood. Luckily, I wasn't bounced into the shooting. Instead, I was instructed to observe the daily habits of an elderly cleaner who worked at Newry's Edward Street RUC station. I quickly discovered that this man was a creature of habit and, as such, the most vulnerable of targets. You could set your watch to his routine. At the same time every morning, he collected the newspapers for the station from Thompsons newsagents in Sugar Island just around the corner. To buy time, I told IRA bosses that the man varied his routine and his route each day, and seemed on a high state of alert. This gave my handlers time to warn the man that his life was in danger. Suddenly, like the milkman, he retired.

Some months later, I spotted the man that I should have shot dead in a different newsagent's in Newry. He was buying sweets for an adoring grandchild. He never knew that, if it hadn't been for me, this child would have been deprived of her grandfather. I felt like a guardian angel.

By now, Sean Mathers had taken over as Newry OC. Back in 1986, I had used my ice-cream van to smuggle a revolver to him on behalf of Conor. It seemed like several lifetimes ago. Mathers and a man called Matty 'Hitchy' Hillen had hatched a plan to blow up soldiers during a charity cycle event.

The route of the so-called Maracycle went past a chapel at a junction on the main Newry to Dundalk road. Every year, army and police patrols tended to loiter around the chapel's black metal railings as it provided an excellent vantage point in several directions.

Days earlier, a piece of black tubular steel containing Semtex had been attached to the railings. It blended in perfectly. A detonating wire had been run down the inside of the tubular steel frame, into a culvert under the road, out the other side of the road and into a wooded area. As it was buried in shallow mud, nobody was going to stumble across this wire. At an appointed time that Sunday, Mathers and Hillen would be standing at the end of that wire, unable to see the church railings and waiting for a signal. Once the signal was given, they would press a detonating button and everybody within 100 yards of those railings would be cut down.

Of course, I tipped off my handlers. The army was thrilled and said it would be pulling out all the stops for this. Nailing Newry's IRA OC in the act of detonating a bomb was considered a massive PR coup.

The task of giving the signal to Mathers and Hillen fell to

a man called Philip and myself. We would be on a high vantage point overlooking the railings – ostensibly watching the Maracycle but really waiting to alert Mathers and Hillen as to when an army patrol was passing. The signal would be relayed to them via CB radio. The agreed word was 'Cortina'. I would be chatting away to them about this and that. As a patrol approached the spot, I was to say, 'My brother's got a new car, it's a Ford ...'

That was the signal to switch on the power. 'What type of Ford?' Mathers would ask.

'It's one of them, oh, what do you call them now, a Ford ... Cortina.'

Bang.

The unit for the operation agreed to meet in the early hours of that morning. There was still work to do and technicalities to be checked. Philip and I waited for Mathers and Hillen for hours. They didn't show. I decided to make a visit to Mathers's home to see what was up. His wife answered the door and said he had been out all night 'on an operation'.

'Some operation,' I mumbled to myself. He had obviously been otherwise engaged.

'Right,' I said to Philip, 'the op is off.'

He agreed and we went home. I was drinking tea when I heard that a bomb attack on the Maracycle had been thwarted and two suspected IRA men arrested. I found out later that Mathers and Hillen turned up late. They had obviously decided to press on with the operation regardless of the lack of support. Clearly, one of the men would be the lookout, the other the 'button-man'. The trouble with having one lookout, as they discovered that morning, is that they can only look in one direction. Mathers and Hillen didn't see the undercover army unit creeping up on them.

Sean Mathers was sentenced to twenty years for conspiracy to murder members of the security forces and conspiracy to cause an explosion. Hillen got twenty-one years.

It was so obvious that the security services knew about the bomb plot. I felt nervous. Only a tiny number of people were privy to this plan. Now top operatives had been arrested. There would be a thorough investigation, probably involving the dreaded IRA internal security unit, the nutting squad. The last thing any volunteer wanted was to be questioned by the nutting squad. They say you're never the same afterwards.

Before that, I would have to write down everything I knew. I would have to detail who I had spoken to in the days leading up to the operation, and on the day of the op itself. In the Provisional IRA, everybody suspected everybody else of being an informant. However, an internal investigation into a compromised op tended to turn the spotlight directly on to those involved. I worried that the nutting squad might start looking at my previous record on operations. I was worried they might detect a pattern.

'Kevin Fulton, a lot of operations you've been involved with have gone badly wrong ...'

The security unit sent down a top operative from Belfast to conduct the inquiry. Apparently, the story that Philip and I told 'sounded like a different operation' to the story told by Mathers and Hillen, which had been sneaked out of prison via coms. Attention soon focused on Mathers and his 'missing hours' in the middle of that night. The man from Belfast suggested to me that Mathers was more afraid of his wife than the Provisional IRA, and left it at that.

I was in the clear. Being completely cleared of any suspicion by the nutting squad emboldened me to take more and more risks. I got wind of an attack being planned on an army patrol in Newry town centre. The team planned to hide a two-kilo Semtex bomb next to a gate in the Patrick Street area of Newry. A detonation wire would be run from the bomb, through a derelict builder's yard, to a quiet backstreet. From here, the bomb would be detonated. The button-men would be in contact by mobile phone with a spotter who would have a good view of the gate. When an army patrol got as close as possible, the spotter would give the verbal signal and the bomb would go off. At least that was the plan.

I told my handlers. The army set up surveillance in the derelict builder's yard. They secretly filmed two IRA men burying the detonation wire in the yard. They observed the men awaiting the signal to press the button. No army patrol came that day. The two button-men were in position again the following afternoon. Again, no army patrol materialised.

The bombers must have been getting suspicious because, the day after that, they started to dismantle the bomb. The army surveillance unit surfaced and the RUC moved in. Jervis Marks, twenty-seven, from Newry was sentenced to fifteen years. Colm Coyle, twenty-two, also from Newry was given fourteen years. The latter had been a member of the Provisional IRA for four months.

I was sure that my information in this instance had saved the lives of British soldiers. I should have felt elated. Instead, I felt a sort of numb exhaustion. My role as a double agent had completely taken over my life. I lived every minute of every day either plotting with the IRA or debriefing my handlers. The rest of the time, I slept only fitfully. I lived every minute of every day with the terror of being shot by a Loyalist death squad or by the SAS. I lived every minute of every day being harassed, threatened and abused by the RUC. They had the manpower and the resources to haunt my every living hour, waking and sleeping. I began to receive death threats on the phone at all hours of the day and night.

'We're getting closer to you, you Provo cunt.'

'Watch your back tomorrow, IRA scum, we're going to fill you with holes.'

Was it any wonder I was finding it hard to sleep?

They raided my home at breakfast, at lunch, at dinnertime. During each and every raid, they expertly rifled through every one of our personal possessions. Whenever I left my home, I was shadowed by one or more police cars. Repeatedly I was stopped and searched, and during every search the seats and spare wheel and anything in the boot would be hurled into a ditch. For the duration of the search, an officer would cover me by pointing a rifle directly at my head. When the search was over, an officer would tell me that they were getting closer. 'And remember,' an old adversary said to me once, 'we only have to be lucky once.'

On completing my journey into town, I would be followed

around on foot, shop to shop. Sometimes, as a little joke, they would ring up the shop manager and inform them that an IRA man was on the premises. I would be followed round by a member of staff until I left.

On the journey home, the whole charade would be repeated.

I felt utterly shattered. Spent. I had been living this life now for ten years, seven days a week. With so many illusions to keep up on so many fronts, I needed to feel strong. Instead, I felt in a state of near mental collapse. I feared that fatigue would make me vulnerable. I couldn't afford to start making mistakes. I desperately needed a long holiday.

I had gone to a job agency called Mivan Overseas with a view to getting some mindless work away from Northern Ireland for a few months. The only skill I could offer was painting, and not the artistic variety. The agency said it would alert me if any short-term contracts came up. I thought I had better mention my plan to Conor. He understood. In fact, he said it was a good idea. He thought I hadn't been myself for a few months. I had seemed strained.

'Go away and sort yourself out,' said Conor.

A painting job came up at Eurodisney in Paris. The contract was for twelve months, with a possible option for an extension. I signed up straight away.

The Provos might have appreciated my urge for a break but, to my amazement, my handlers were far less sympathetic. Bob and Pete, full-time dogs of war, just couldn't comprehend my desperation for complete and utter change. I was holding up their project – or at least that's how they made me feel.

I shrugged off their disapproval and, in August 1991, headed out to Paris. My task was to paint the Big Thunder Mountain theme ride. The days were long and tedious – just what I needed. By the end of the first week, the tension that had strangled my every thought and feeling and action for so long had melted away. Fresh air, sunshine, a straightforward task – I felt euphoric. I felt like I had just stepped off Big Thunder Mountain after a ride lasting ten years.

I started to imagine life free of the Provisional IRA and free of British intelligence. I started to imagine normal life. Perhaps this was what my handlers were scared of – that I would get a taste for it and want more, that I would quit my role as a double agent and get my life back. As every day passed, I became increasingly attuned to normality. I felt myself being lured away from my old life of lightning meetings and clandestine phone calls and murderous plotting. Trust fate to spoil my Damascene moment.

I was relaxing in my living quarters one Sunday afternoon, two weeks into my contract, when my phone rang. It was my wife. 'Have you seen the papers?' she asked.

'Hardly,' I said. 'Where would I find the Irish papers in Eurodisney?'

'Try to get a copy of the *Sunday Express*,' she said. 'You're on the front page.'

'What?'

'Get a copy,' she said. 'You'll have to see it to believe it.'

I got a fellow workman to drive me to a newsagent's near the city. I picked up a copy of the *Express* and baulked at the headline: IRA INFILTRATE DISNEYLAND. I read on feverishly.

The *Sunday Express* reported that it had identified 'prominent' IRA members amongst the 600 people employed at Eurodisney, including 'some with convictions for serious terrorist offences'. It named three: Joe Haughey, John Gillen and Kevin Fulton, 'a prominent Provo from Newry'.

I paid for the paper and got back to the living quarters as quickly as possible. I decided to seek out my fellow 'prominent IRA men'. I tracked down Joe Haughey on the other side of the workers' compound. He was a big man with large, rounded shoulders, missing teeth and a flushed face. He read the paper with his mouth wide open. 'How the fuck ...?' he said in a strong Belfast accent.

We sat in his room and chatted. Haughey hailed from the notorious Unity Walk in west Belfast, and was known as the Hawk from the Walk. He had survived several seven-day detentions in RUC interrogation centres and so had a catchphrase: 'The Hawk from the Walk don't talk.' He made no secret of his IRA connections and nor did I. What was the point?

A week or so later, we were dismissed from our jobs. I headed back to Newry and into the arms of my handlers. I couldn't contain my anger. They seemed delighted. 'Look at it this way,' said Pete, 'it's great for your cover, and it's helped you befriend a leading Belfast Provo. It's worked out quite well.'

It would be many years later before I'd find out the truth about the *Sunday Express* story. The security services tipped off the newspaper about the presence of Joe Haughey and myself at Eurodisney. They deliberately leaked the story to the *Express* to force me back to Northern Ireland, and back into my role as a double agent. Little did I know just how much I was being manipulated by my handlers, men who I trusted so much.

Perhaps they knew that the IRA was about to give me a promotion.

CHAPTER EIGHT

I t took a few seconds for Conor's words to register.
I was driving towards a blazing low early-morning sun,
squinting hard. I sensed Conor watching me expectantly
from the passenger seat. He had been acting cagey, and a
little smug, since I had picked him up from an IRA safe house
earlier. Was it the sun dazzling me, or the shock of Conor's
announcement?

'You've been chosen to become a member of the security
unit.'

The security unit, the IRA's internal police, the nutting
squad, charged with rooting out and killing informants and
double agents. Christ, I thought to myself. Some supernatural
force is mocking me now.

I could sense Conor scrutinising my face. He must have
read my look of disbelief. Perhaps he assumed I was

struggling to register the shock of such a sudden yet glorious promotion. 'Well,' said Conor, 'what do you think?'

'Yeah,' I said vaguely, maintaining a nonchalant façade. Inside, thoughts strobed through my mind quicker than the white road-lines flashing under my car. I thought I had better say something. 'So how would it work?'

'Well,' said Conor, 'me and Niall are basically the security unit for Dundalk, Armagh and South Down. We handle things in our area, though of course we come under the command of the main IRA security unit in Belfast. Anything serious and they get involved. You'll be meeting some of the main players from Belfast.'

'Right,' I said. I could certainly see the benefits to this. The IRA's power base was in Belfast. Getting involved with senior IRA men from there would put me at the very heart of the IRA. My handlers would be thrilled. But what exactly would I have to do to gain the keys to this black kingdom?

'We vet new recruits,' said Conor, 'we debrief volunteers who have been interrogated by the security forces, find out if they've talked and, if so, what they've said. Of course, this is a breach of discipline. You'll be part of any inquiry into breaches of discipline.'

I couldn't bring myself to ask the question I really wanted to ask. I knew Conor would get to it eventually. 'Anyone suspected of breaking the rules of the Green Book, you'll be part of the team that'll find out the truth of the matter. And you could find yourself having to punish transgressors. Volunteers might be suspended. They might get a court martial and be expelled ...'

I bit my lip. The bottom line was coming.

'Sometimes people will have to be punished. You may have to dole out the punishment yourself. You might find yourself carrying out punishment shootings, Kevin,' said Conor, still scrutinising my face. 'Think you're up to it?'

'Oh yeah,' I said, 'damn right I'm up to it.'

'And then there are informers,' Conor went on animatedly. Clearly, he loved working for the security unit. 'Sometimes they get an amnesty, but, where a death sentence is recommended by the court of inquiry, a member of the Army Council makes the final decision.'

I turned to see Conor relishing the moment, smiling at me as if I had won some sort of prize.

'You could find yourself executing touts.'

My arms were a dead weight on the steering wheel. I realised I had been in a sort of trance for several minutes, driving on autopilot as if I was no longer in control of the car. Somewhere along the line, it had taken over. My head was bulging.

A punishment shooting was one thing. Shooting dead a man with his hands tied behind his back, begging for mercy, was an altogether different proposition. I knew that, by accepting this promotion, I could be ordered at any time to stiff a tout after a kangaroo court. There would be no time to ring handlers, no time to ensure some dastardly stroke of ill-fortune scupper the crime in hand. Surely, I thought, surely my handlers won't sanction this promotion. Surely, it was time for me to disappear.

I couldn't have been more wrong.

'This is a remarkable breakthrough,' said Bob from MI5.

'This is precisely why you were hand picked for this job. You are now in the inner circle. Well done!'

'Think about it,' said Pete. 'You'll be meeting some of the main players from Belfast. Some of the absolute top men. You'll be close to the real movers and shakers, the people who sanction the real major-league stuff.'

'You want to stop an atrocity?' said Bob. 'Well, it's only by getting in with these people that you can even become party to operations of that scale.'

'But what if I have to execute someone?' I said. 'I mean, surely this is overstepping the mark.'

'No, look,' said Bob, 'we've managed to get other people into positions like this. Use your common sense. If it isn't you putting the bullet into that tout's head, it'll be someone else. At least you know that somewhere down the line, it'll pay off for us. You must think of the bigger picture. If you don't do it, someone else will. There's no point trying to save any of these people anyhow. They're only IRA scum after all.'

'Another IRA person gets shot,' said Pete, 'so what? Another dead Provie is hardly bad news for anyone, is it? And it's the ultimate cover for you. Who'd ever suspect that someone executing informants is an agent?'

The message was clear – the priority for my handlers was saving their colleagues in the army and the RUC. Their secondary concern was saving innocent people. They didn't give a damn about anyone else. I suppose this had been obvious for some time and came as no real surprise. What did surprise me though was Bob's admission that they had other agents at this level within the IRA. Were these men still active in the organisation? How many were there? Were they planting bombs and shooting people on behalf of British intelligence?

For the first time, I began to wonder who controlled people like my handlers. I began to wonder if, to them and their colleagues in MI5 and the Force Research Unit, Northern Ireland was one big elaborate playground where they had carte blanche to do exactly as they pleased. They seemed a law unto themselves.

I began to wonder who was running the war in Northern Ireland. I began to wonder if it was in anyone's interest for the war to cease. Without the conflict, what would people like Bob from MI5, Pete from military intelligence or Conor do with themselves? If the war ended, so would their power, status and influence.

'You've got to do it,' said Bob. 'We've gone too far to pull out now.'

'Do it,' said Pete. 'Give it a few weeks and we'll see how it goes. We can always pull you out if it gets too hot.'

I decided to go along with it just as I had decided to go along with everything since I had become a double agent – reluctantly and in a state of utter dependency. I relied on someone else making the decision for me, and someone else saving me if it all went wrong.

Perhaps my handlers sensed my gloom. At our next secret rendezvous, they announced a new improved pay deal. Bob detailed our lucrative new arrangement in the manner of an indulgent sugar daddy. 'Your basic will stay the same, £130 per week in your hand. But we're going to put £300 per week into a secret savings account which you can access once your career as a double agent comes to an end,' said Bob.

Pete took up the reins. 'Any time your information ends in a conviction, we'll put a lump sum into your account. The amount will depend on who has been convicted, but, if it's a known IRA man, you'll get between five and ten grand. Not bad, eh?'

'Not bad at all,' I said grinning. After all, this was one job with no pension scheme and no real future.

Their largesse didn't end there. I was handed a bag stuffed full of banknotes. 'There's five thousand in there,' said Bob. 'This is to pay for your new car. It's waiting for you at a garage near London. You're expected to pick it up later this week.'

'They won't accept Northern Ireland notes,' I said, speaking from previous experience.

'Oh, this garage will,' said Pete knowingly.

I was handed my itinerary – fly into Luton Airport, hire a car and drive to a garage in Dagenham, Essex. There I'd ask for a man called Bob. Bob would hand me the keys to the car – a year-old Peugeot 405 – in exchange for the cash. I asked them if I could take along my brother-in-law. I could use a map-reader, and some company. He also knew a bit about cars, so I figured I could get some cash knocked off. They agreed.

A few days later, I was presented with two one-way tickets to Luton Airport and two ferry tickets from Stranraer in Scotland to Larne, near Belfast.

Amongst my IRA cronies, travelling to England to buy a

car aroused no suspicions. Lots of people bought cars on the mainland at that time, simply because second-hand models tended to be cheaper and of better quality.

As usual, I got stopped at the airport. That was one of the down sides to being an IRA man. After the standard strip search and verbal abuse, I was asked what I was doing with five thousand pounds in cash. I told them I was buying a car, but they were having none of it.

'No garage over here will take Northern Ireland notes!' said a customs man triumphantly, and I had to laugh.

After more than an hour of detainment, I was allowed to make a phone call. I called my handlers. To my amazement, they had already been alerted to my presence at Luton Airport. Of course, they couldn't tell airport officials that I was travelling at their behest. Instead, my handlers told HM Customs thay would arrange to get a surveillance unit to tail me from the airport, and asked them to hold me at the airport for another hour.

'Don't worry,' said Pete, 'we've told the garage you're going to be a few hours late.'

'Can you not do something about this,' I said, for I was truly sick of being harassed.

'We can't tell them to let you go, can we?' barked Pete. 'They'd smell a rat then, wouldn't they? Word would get out. It wouldn't look too good for you, would it? Being miraculously released after a phone call. No, no, we've got to play the game.'

'No, no, no, Pete,' I said sarcastically, '*I*'ve got to play the game. You just sit on your fat arse.'

DOUBLE AGENT

I hung up and counted down the minutes to my release. I struggled to keep up the smiles and the smart-arse wisecracks. I was growing very weary of this game.

Finally, I got out. It seemed no time until a skyscape of pencil-thin high-rise blocks announced Dagenham. Our appointed garage was just off a main road. As instructed, I asked for Bob.

Bob was bald and cagey. I said I was looking for a car.

'How much?' he said.

'Five grand,' I said.

'This one will suit you,' said Bob, leading me to a grey Peugeot 405.

It was immaculate. Low mileage. One previous owner. I figured it was worth a good deal more than five thousand. So did my brother-in-law. Whenever Bob wasn't looking, he would lean into my ear and say, 'You're getting it for nothing!' I was sure Bob could hear him. Some fucking negotiator, I remember thinking.

'Five grand, you say?' I said.

'Five,' said Bob.

'Four six,' I ventured.

'Five,' said Bob.

'Four eight,' I said, smiling.

'Five,' said Bob, not smiling.

'Ah, c'mon,' I said, 'you've got to give me some slack!'

He remained stony faced.

'What about five two?' I said.

My brother-in-law coughed dramatically.

'Five,' said Bob.

168

'Five four? I tell you what, I'll give you six!'

'Five,' said Bob, eyeing me to say in no uncertain terms that he wasn't enjoying this particular game one bit.

'Agreed,' I said, mock-spitting into the palm of my hand. By the time I offered it, Bob was halfway to his office.

'What the fuck are you playing at?' gasped my brother-in-law.

All the way to Stranraer, my driving partner wondered aloud why Bob had let the car go so cheap, while I wondered privately what the catch might be to this amazing deal. I soon found out.

As Bob and Pete ran through the car's clandestine functions, I felt like James Bond being briefed by Q. The car contained a satellite tracking device and a bug. Both had been hidden deep within the car's dashboard. 'You'd have to strip the entire car to find anything suspicious,' explained Pete, 'so don't worry about the police or the army coming across anything during a search. It won't happen.'

The tape recorder was controlled by two tiny pins under the steering wheel. One switch activated a microphone, the other the bug itself, which recorded every word uttered inside the car. My handlers urged me to lend the car to my IRA connections at every given opportunity, and to be sure to alert them whenever I did.

It was in my new car, with the bug activated, that I told Conor I was willing to join the security unit. Just for the record, I asked him again what my duties would be. I then insisted he tell me about the occasions when he had executed touts.

My first task as a fully fledged member of the nutting squad was to observe Conor vetting three new recruits. One by one, they gave the same reasons for wanting to join: they had been harassed by the police; a family member had been insulted/injured/killed by the British army; they were sick of being victimised for being Catholic by the British State; they wanted to even things up – why should Protestants get the best jobs and houses? Each one of them expressed complete and utter disillusionment with the status quo, and alienation from their own society. I realised that the Provisional IRA benefited from a fathomless pool of potential recruits. I realised that, to stop people dying, we would first have to give them good reasons to live.

Conor asked them all the same questions. Had they any known links with Sinn Fein or the IRA? Had they attended Republican marches or funerals? Had they criminal records?

I found myself wondering if I could bring myself to execute one of these men. Suppose they confessed to being a tout? Could I administer the ultimate sanction, at the behest of an IRA kangaroo court? Listening to these men's voices, hearing about their disenfranchised lives, I came to the conclusion that I just couldn't do it. What would happen to me if I bottled it? A refusal to kill would invite derision and, worse still, suspicion. All my hard-earned credibility would be dashed at a stroke. By now, my thinking was so skewed I decided that maybe cold-blooded murder would be a natural progression for me. Maybe, in time, it would become run-of-the-mill, once I'd kneecapped a few people first.

I felt confident that, if presented with absolutely no chance of escape, I could bring myself to administer IRA-style justice by shooting a bullet through the knee of a transgressor. I assumed that the victim would inevitably be someone I disliked – a terrorist or a drug dealer. And I assumed that the victim would have had ample warning to cease doing whatever it was that earned the wrath of the IRA.

In short, I thought that people who got kneecapped deserved it.

I was to discover that I was wrong.

To senior members of the IRA, ordering a punishment shooting was easier than ordering a pizza. In the IRA's arena of justice, the local sheriff was all powerful and any OC or senior IRA member could order a kneecapping, for any reason, without fear of censure. As a result, punishment shootings were doled out to anyone whose face didn't fit. Knees were crippled purely to settle scores.

The first time I was bounced into a punishment shooting showed just how petty these scores could be. I got the phone call early in the evening. From the tone of the voice on the other end of the line, you would think I was being dispatched to post a letter.

'Fly up the road there,' said a Provisional IRA OC, who for legal reasons I will refer to as Paul, 'and meet me outside the Corner Bar in Rostrevor.'

I arrived to find Paul and another man waiting in a car. I noticed both had AK-47s resting on their laps. I looked at the weapons with horror. It's bad enough to be hit with a 9mm bullet, but an AK-47 was more likely to blow your leg off than make 'a nice neat little hole', as Conor was wont to put it. The men nodded as if to say, 'Don't start asking questions', pulled down their balaclavas and got out of the car. I pulled my mask down and followed them through the front door of the pub. It was quiet; it became even quieter when we were spotted.

Paul approached two young fellows at the bar. Both appeared to be in their early twenties. I felt myself sighing. The pair bolted to their feet at once. One word from Paul and they didn't even look at each other before walking expectantly to the front door. Once outside, Paul told the men to put their hands on their heads and walk round the corner of the pub. I prayed they wouldn't make a run for it. A pair of AK-47s would make a right mess if unleashed on a couple of runners.

Slowly, the two men walked round the corner, the three of us following. I awaited the next order. I expected Paul to tell the two men to stop and turn around. Instead, two rounds rang out, hitting the men as they still walked. Blood burst, slapping the walls in loud splats. The squealing didn't sound human. We turned casually and strolled back to our cars, as though we had just taken a leak. I really wanted to run. I stole a look back. One man was writhing on the ground, the other hopping about. Gingerly, one or two heads peeked out of the pub's front door.

'Shouldn't we call an ambulance?' I said.

'Already done,' said the second masked man.

I climbed into my car and took one more look at the two men, now being tended to by the pub regulars. The scene was surreally calm, as if it had replayed itself a hundred times before. The two men, howling like maimed dogs, were never going to recover fully from the attack, mentally or physically. For the rest of their lives, every step they took would punish them anew for their misdemeanour.

So what was their heinous crime?

It was a day or two later before I found out. Both belonged to a one-time Republican family. However, it wasn't the softening of the family's political standpoint that earned the wrath of the IRA. Apparently, the family had been accused of stealing some scrap metal from the garden of an IRA man – a crime deemed to be of sufficient gravity to warrant a punishment shooting with a pair of AK-47s.

That night, I took another long, hard look at myself in the mirror. I knew that, for the benefit of my reputation within the IRA, and for the amusement of my fellow volunteers, I would have to turn this horrific incident into a funny story. A witty anecdote. A belly laugh. I knew I would have to think up some good one-liners.

I looked at the stranger staring back at me and took a long breath. I told this stranger that he was a British soldier on a very special mission. 'You've got to go on,' I told him over and over, 'you're saving lives.'

The next recipient of IRA justice was a thief. Of course, the Provisional IRA didn't object to thieving in principle. What senior IRA men did object to was someone stealing something from them, or stealing and not paying their cut.

Nobody told me exactly which of these crimes the man was guilty of. All I was told was that he was a 'tea leaf', and that this was all I needed to know. Trouble was, I already knew the man. He was small fry, a petty crook. Clearly, this was another personal vendetta, a score to be settled or a reputation to be upheld – all under the veneer of IRA 'housekeeping'.

Six of us got bounced into the operation. After the punishment shooting that 'went wrong' in 1990, resulting in the death of an ex-IRA man, it was decided to tackle future assignments with a single weapon but with plenty of back-up. Apart from ensuring the safety of the volunteers, a show of strength spread more fear and terror. The Provisional IRA was in the business of spreading terror. It was also a good excuse to bring along some raw recruits and impress them with a display of IRA justice in action.

The trigger-man was handed a Webley .455 for the job. Once again, I was flabbergasted by the choice of weapon. The gun was a weighty, ungainly contraption that fired lead bullets the size of bean cans. The volunteer carrying the gun joked that to fire it he would need someone else to hold the barrel. I dreaded the mess and wondered aloud why we weren't given appropriate weapons for these assignments. It was not as if the Provisional IRA was suffering a shortage of revolvers.

We pulled up outside the house. Quietly we clambered out and shuffled to the front door. At this moment, in the black silence, the butterflies did a quick practice lap around my stomach. After all, I didn't quite know what to expect. It was a drab two-storey home with no doorbell, so I rapped on the frosted glass of the front door. A child answered.

'We're from the Irish Republican Army,' came a voice, and in we barged.

The front room was packed with the man's children. Each of them froze stiff at the sight of us. Questions about the whereabouts of their daddy were met with ghostly stares. They were herded quietly into the living room. The plan was to babysit them there while the father took a couple of bullets in another room. Two of us slipped upstairs to seek him out.

We crept along a landing, floorboards creaking beneath us. Quietly I pushed in the first door. Nothing. As we felt our way along the black hallway, a series of unmistakable sounds came from another room. Light framed the door. I nodded to my accomplice. We crept towards that light and the sounds got louder.

As I pushed open the door to the master bedroom, the couple on the bed remained oblivious to our presence. As if entering a family home armed and masked wasn't a sufficient violation, we now found ourselves strolling in on a married couple sharing a private moment. I felt mortified. Clearly, we couldn't leave the room and wait until they had completed their liaison. It would have been foolhardy to take my eyes off him at all. So, like some flustered butler, I coughed politely.

He froze. Ever so slowly, he turned his face towards me. 'What the fuck ...?' he said, hopping to his feet and grabbing his privates. His wife grabbed at a sheet.

I decided I needed to sound firmer. 'We're from the IRA,' I said to the wide-eyed, naked man before me. 'Put something on and come downstairs.' As he climbed into a pair of white underpants in record time, I turned to his wife. 'And you'd better put something on too.'

Still wrapped in the sheet, she rose and made for her dressing gown hanging on a wardrobe door. As she went to put it on, the two masked IRA men in her bedroom looked away. This was a very Catholic crime.

Dressed in only his underpants, he led the way downstairs. I followed, feeling like the director of some particularly sick and degrading pageant. Self-disgust swelled within me. As usual, I hid it by joining in with the puerile sniggering and the lewd comments aimed at the red-faced couple as they were led to their kitchen.

Over and over, they asked after the kids.

'They're all right,' I said. 'They're in the sitting room, safe and sound.'

'We want the keys to your van, that's all,' said one of the masked men. Putting him at ease was the plan. In a house full of kids, the last thing you wanted was a gunman running round after a man wearing only underpants.

'Sit down here,' said the gunman to him, nodding towards a pine bench next to a breakfast table. 'Listen carefully,' he went on, 'you've got twenty-four hours to get out of Ireland.' With that, a shot rang out.

Suddenly, he was hopping up and down on one leg, howling, his wife screaming, blood chasing across the lino. Another shot sounded. We all jumped as it bounced off the radiator behind him with a great clank. He was pogoing up and down so violently that the gunman completely missed him with a second shot. Now I could hear the kids screaming. It was time to bail out. We trooped out to the van and sped off.

It was always the next day, when the adrenaline had

levelled out, that the full horror of what I had been involved in hit home. The heady cocktail of guilt and shock made for the most debilitating hangover. To a soldier trained in warfare, these punishments seemed so cowardly and unjustified. A few days later, the injustice of this particular punishment shooting was confirmed. Out of the blue, the IRA reversed the expulsion order against him. Apparently, an IRA friend of his put in a good word with Conor and that was that.

This proved to me that IRA justice wasn't administered on the basis of what a person did or didn't do. It was dished out to those who weren't connected to the gilded circle, to those whose faces didn't fit. The IRA was the playground bully and I was his sneaky little helper.

However, the IRA wasn't finished with this family just yet.

A few months later, I was part of a team dispatched to punish his brother who happened to live near by. The front door was locked so I knocked. He emerged into a glass porch. He took one look at the team of masked men waiting for him and elected not to open up. He was turning to go back in when the glass shattered. I think I heard three shots. The dark-red bloodied holes in his ankles suggested he had been hit twice. I was able to make such a cold, detached forensic observation because I was growing used to people writhing about in pools of their own blood, squealing like pigs.

In all, I played roles of varying significance in six punishment shootings. To protect myself against legal proceedings, and to protect my family members against reprisals, I can't go into detail. The Good Friday Agreement protects terrorists, but it doesn't protect agents who murdered and maimed in the name of the British Crown. I can't go into the detail, but I can describe my transformation into a ruthlessly robotic IRA operative.

I was so far gone by this stage – so hardened to barbarism, so de-programmed of natural human compassion – that the kneecapping of some lowlife IRA man or criminal associate didn't really play on my conscience. I had convinced myself that anyone who aligned themselves to the IRA probably deserved anything they got. After all, I doubted if they shed tears over children killed by bombs or innocent workers slaughtered for doing their jobs. Why should I be tormented by feelings of guilt when dealing with people who never seemed to flinch from committing barbarous acts? I was now hardened to violence and this suited me fine. At least now I could look these IRA killers in the eye and beat them on their own terms. Or could I? The big test was still to come. And come it did. I was soon ordered to attend my first court of inquiry.

A shipment of arms bound for the IRA had been found by the British army at a butcher's shop in Castlewellan, near Newcastle in County Down; it had fallen through into the shop from the flat above. Everyone involved in the importation had been questioned. However, the nutting squad was still not satisfied. One volunteer in particular had failed to convince his interrogators that he was telling them everything he knew. He was facing an IRA court martial. The security unit's top men from Belfast were on their way down to conduct the show.

I was given the task of preparing a location for the court martial. A contact in Belfast rang me to arrange a meeting. There, he furnished me with the address where the court martial was to take place, a family home in Omeath. I was told that the home had hosted interrogations in the past. I will always remember what the Belfast man told me next. 'There should be a roll of plastic floor-covering in the garage,' he said matter-of-factly. 'Can you check it out? If there isn't, can you get hold of some?'

'Sure,' I said, and I shuddered at the humdrum practicality of death. The plastic covering could be for one thing only – to gather all the damning traces of forensic evidence in the event of an execution. The blood, the pieces of skull, the brains.

'Good,' said the man from Belfast. 'We don't want to be ruining their floors.'

It was my first real operational contact with the Belfast IRA – a small but hugely significant development which my handlers would appreciate. I collected three days' groceries and brought them to the house. I then set to work. I blacked out all windows visible to the world at large. We required one room for the interrogation, so I picked a medium-sized bedroom at the back of the house. Piece by piece, I took out all the furniture and stored it in the room next door, save for a single wooden chair. I hung a black drape on the window so that the room was dark and gloomy, but not pitch black. I positioned the chair so that it faced the empty wall. I sat in it to check it was solid. It was. I stared straight ahead at the wall. Just like they told you in the Green Book lectures, I picked a spot and stared hard. An icy draught played across my neck, making my shoulders fidget. The spot on the wall wavered and started inching closer. I felt hot now, hot and immobile, rooted to the chair. Helpless. I wanted to get up and leave this room instantly, but I didn't feel able. It was as if my subconscious was forcing me to confront my greatest fear: was this a premonition of the fate that awaited me?

I don't know how long I sat there, transfixed by this fatalistic glimpse of terror, but I completely forgot to check if there was any floor-covering left in the garage. Fortunately, there was a roll left over from a previous interrogation. It seemed this house was used regularly.

The following morning, I picked up Conor and Niall in a hire van. The man facing court martial over the intercepted arms shipment was to be waiting for us outside a hotel in Killeen.

'He'll hardly turn up, will he?' I said.

'Oh, he will,' laughed Conor. 'He's no idea he's facing an interrogation. He thinks he's heading down south with us for a few days. To a training camp!'

They both laughed.

'The only place this poor fucker's going is down a hole!' added Niall.

More laughter.

'What?' I said. 'He's been found guilty?'

'He talked, so he's facing court martial. The only thing left is to decide what happens to him,' said Conor. 'I'm one of the three judges and I've made up my mind.' With that, he mimicked the action of firing a revolver.

Niall laughed delightedly.

I shuddered silently as I considered how men like this could be granted the ultimate power of life over death.

When I pulled into the car park of the hotel, I was disappointed to see the poor man standing there, his travel bag at his feet as if he were going on holiday. As we approached, he smiled and waved at the van in case we might have missed him. I found myself laughing now. This was happening to me more and more lately. Where once such a sight would have thoroughly depressed me, it now made me howl with laughter. I was developing a taste for the very blackest of comedy. After all, I knew only too well that at best this man would be dismissed from the IRA in disgrace. He would be forced to leave his family and friends and life in Northern Ireland, and suffer a life of paranoid exile in the Republic. However, when weighed up against the alternative option – his body found in a ditch, a black bin-liner for a shroud – he would happily settle for exile.

He was about thirty, and so broad that he struggled to get into the car. He greeted us all warmly and began to chatter. Clearly, he didn't suspect a thing. I watched in the rear-view mirror as Niall pulled out a gun.

'We're from the security unit,' said Niall sharply. 'Keep quiet.'

Cable ties were slapped on to his wrists. The reason for cable ties was explained to me later – in the event of us coming across an army or police roadblock, the cuffs could be cut off quickly with a pair of scissors. The security forces would be none the wiser. I felt like telling them that the security forces would be only too happy to see an IRA security unit hauling a volunteer off to exile or, better still, death.

We parked up in the well-hidden rear yard of the house in Omeath. I followed the condemned man, Niall and Conor into the interrogation room. There, two men stood waiting. It was clear from the outset who was boss. Fat, but with a bolt-upright military gait, he looked every inch a British army officer. However, one thing gave his true role away: a copy of the IRA's Green Book tucked under his right arm. As I found out later, he was John Joe Magee from Belfast, and head of the nutting squad. I cannot reveal the identity of the other man, so I will give him the name Michael, notorious to all volunteers as the security unit's most ruthless interrogator, and the IRA's most zealous dispenser of 'justice'.

The condemned man walked in and, without being asked, sat on the chair facing the wall. In his Sunday-best jumper and ironed slacks, he looked like a man set to endure nothing more arduous than a game of golf. The chair was way too small for his frame, so he sat hunched up like an overgrown schoolboy, breathing heavily. Conor indicated that I should leave. He followed me to the hallway and told me to be at the pier in Omeath, just down the road, in two hours' time. I said I would head there directly and wait.

I got to the pier and surveyed the breathtaking view of Carlingford Lough. I breathed the air in deeply. Seeing that wretched man hunched up in his seat made me appreciate being alive. I started to wonder if I would ever be in that position, sitting on a chair facing a wall, wondering if I would ever see my wife and family again. I comforted myself with the knowledge that Bob and Pete would pull me out long before such a scenario ever came about. That was my salvation, for I knew I wouldn't be able to withstand a concentrated IRA interrogation. Who could?

Conor turned up early and told me the interrogation would continue the next day. The man had made certain admissions and, to Conor's apparent delight, was 'going down a hole'.

He waited until I started the engine, then said casually, 'This might be your first execution.'

A knot of dread set like concrete in my stomach.

I was now well used to maintaining a façade of impenetrable hardness. My tone didn't alter when I asked, 'How is it decided, you know, who pulls the trigger?'

'Well, he's local so it's going to be you, me or Niall. We'll find some way of deciding,' said Conor.

I unwound the window for some air. I desperately wanted to see the angles. Perhaps Conor was toying with me, testing me. I simply had to keep up the charade, at least for today. At least until I received instruction from my handlers.

That night I drove to a phone box a few miles outside Newry and dialled my exclusive hotline number to my handlers. Eventually, I got through to Pete. As ever, he made my dilemma seem banal. He rolled out the usual justifications. If the man's going to get a bullet in his head anyway, what difference did it make who pulled the trigger? He made it clear that he was not going to pull me out on an outside chance that I *might* be ordered to kill an IRA volunteer. I was a soldier. I had been trained to kill.

This man was the enemy. What could be more straight-forward? What difference would it make if he had his hands tied behind his back? By executing this 'murdering shit', I would become utterly trusted by the Provisional IRA's elite. 'Surely that's worth dispatching a bullet into the head of some IRA hoodlum.'

With no obvious way out, I convinced myself that Conor was testing my resolve. I had bluffed him out many times in the past, and I knew I could do it again. The following morning I returned to the pier at Omeath to meet him. Conor arrived at about half past ten with a com. It was to be delivered to an address in South Armagh. The man's answers would be compared in minute detail to the answers he gave the previous week, and measured against the testimony of the other volunteers involved in the arms dump. It was a simple but devastatingly effective way of catching out a liar. I looked at the tiny piece of paper wrapped in cling film and saw a bullet.

After delivering the com, I returned to the picturesque little family home that doubled up as an IRA interrogation centre. Conor beckoned me in and led me into a garage. 'Here, give me a hand,' he said. He was unfolding plastic floor-covering. I grabbed one end and helped him lay it out on the garage floor. This could mean one thing only: the man was about to be executed here in the garage.

Niall strolled in.

'Well?' said Conor expectantly.

'Still waiting,' said Niall.

'Waiting for what?' I said.

'The nod from on high,' said Conor, and they pulled faces of mock boredom.

'The decision to execute a tout has to come from someone on the Army Council,' said Niall. 'We're waiting for the nod from South Armagh to give us the go-ahead.'

'I wouldn't anticipate any problem there,' said Conor. 'So who's up for it?'

I smiled as hard as I could. I noticed a glint in Conor's eye. As ever, Niall looked as cold as a snake. 'Straws?' suggested Niall.

'Sounds good to me,' I said.

With that, Conor called in a Belfast volunteer (who I'll call Sean), who'd arrived with McGee that morning. Sean went back into the house. Seconds later, he returned. With a dramatic flourish worthy of a magician, he proffered his left hand, clenched into a fist. In the fleshy gap between thumb and fingers stood the ends of three cocktail sticks, equal in length. One was cut short at the other hidden end. Whoever pulled that short stick would have to stiff the big man here in the garage.

Niall said he would go first. You didn't argue with Niall. He ran his finger through the space above the three ends like a psychic. He settled on the middle stick. Slowly, and with the gentle precision of a surgeon, he started to pull. The stick came and came and came. It wouldn't be Niall.

Conor looked at me with a thin smile. 'Go on,' he said, 'you go.'

Time stopped still. Seconds groaned by like whole days. I wondered if the others could hear my heart pounding. The beats were reverberating in the small of my ears. Fuck it, I thought in a fatalistic way, here goes. I went for the left stick. It felt stiff in Sean's hand. I pulled it out with the dread of a man pulling a pin out of a faulty hand grenade.

It was long.

Sean opened his fist to reveal the last, shortened stick. Conor would be the executioner. He acted as if he'd won the pools. Of course, I should have known that he would react in such a gung-ho fashion, so I feigned disappointment. I told them I was really looking forward to 'stiffing a tout' and, in their warped minds, they couldn't imagine why I would feel otherwise. I followed them back into the house and ducked into the bathroom. I leaned over the sink, splashed my face with water, stared at my image in the mirror and said a thank you to God. However, I knew I was on borrowed time. I couldn't keep abusing my luck. How long could I carry on without being either found out or forced to kill someone in cold blood? Fate wasn't so much closing in on me as wrapping its cold fingers around my throat.

Minutes later, the verdict came from on high. The man was to be spared. He was dismissed from the IRA in disgrace and ordered to go into exile immediately. Conor and Niall just couldn't understand why. Such was the arbitrary nature of IRA justice that, on another day, this man would have been down a hole.

So why didn't I bail out after this narrow escape? Because I felt like I had no choice but to carry on. It was like being stuck on a runaway train: there was no turning back and no easy way off, yet I knew that I was destined to hit the buffers at some point. Despite this, at times I revelled in the insane rush of the journey. Having spent the last ten years living like this, how could I return to normal life? How could I get a proper job? How could I explain to a potential employer what I had been doing for the previous decade? Besides, I felt that, as I moved up through the ranks of the IRA, I was getting closer to my reward of a new life away from Northern Ireland.

I knew my employers would only make good their promise to relocate me if I landed a really big prize for them. It might sound reckless, but I felt that, if I could earn the trust of men like John Joe Magee, I would soon really be able to damage the Provisional IRA. My handlers agreed, and they dangled the carrot of a new life before me at every opportunity. They led me to believe that I was on the verge of earning my escape from this madness. I really hoped this was the case. I knew I couldn't carry on indefinitely living this way.

I threw myself into my work for the nutting squad. Over the following months, I sat in on four interrogations. Thankfully, none ended in an execution, but I did get to know some of the major players from Belfast. I formed a particularly close bond with Magee, the man I have called Michael and another Belfast provie I have called Sean.

I came to learn that, like me, John Joe Magee had served in the British army. He had been in the Special Boat Squadron of the Royal Marines, no less. Though aged in his mid-fifties, overweight and a heavy smoker, Magee cut an impressive figure. He had a rare presence and tended to dominate a room. We swapped army anecdotes like old pals. It quickly became clear to me that, in his capacity as an IRA man, he had been deprived of the chance to talk freely and openly about his army days. He seemed genuinely grateful for the opportunity.

That was Magee the person. Magee the witch-hunter-in-chief was an altogether more formidable and terrifying beast. I watched him in action on several occasions, debriefing IRA men who had been interrogated by the RUC, and quizzing suspected touts. His thoroughness was what impressed me most. He set out to find the truth and, with an attention to detail that bordered on the pathological, he inevitably got to it. If Magee got even the faintest whiff of duplicity, he went after it like a bloodhound. People broke under the sheer pressure of his thoroughness. It was easy to see how he had risen to become head of the nutting squad.

Michael was Magee's ambitious lieutenant. He was small in stature, yet his reputation within the IRA was legendary. While Magee went obsessively in search of the truth, Michael seemed interested only in someone's guilt. Michael thought nothing of promising an amnesty to an informant during a court of inquiry, only to then renege on that deal once the accused had confessed. I wondered how many volunteers had been duped in this way and then paid with their lives. It seemed the lowest of low tricks.

He had a favourite story about one such victim (a now legendary story, which he told to many). After being offered an amnesty, the man confessed all. He assured the man that he had nothing to worry about. To show there were no hard feelings, he even insisted on driving him home. On arriving at the man's home, Michael told him to keep his blindfold on for security reasons, and offered to guide him to his front door. He found the man's pathetic stumbling hilarious. He even mimicked his voice as he struggled along. 'Is this my house now? Is this my house now?'

'No, not yet, keep going, you've to go a bit further yet.'

When the man had been lured around the corner to a secluded spot, Michael shot him in the head. He wasn't setting an example to other potential informants – the two men were the only people there. He did it purely for his own pleasure.

In a strange way, there were very few people in the Provisional IRA for whom I felt genuine loathing and fear.

He was one of them.

CHAPTER NINE

Getting inside the Belfast wing of the Provisional IRA was the holy grail for me and my handlers. This was the power base of the organisation, after all. It was right there, in the black heart of the beast, that we would be able to wreak most damage.

With men like Michael, John Joe Magee and Tony Hughes to vouch for me, I set about getting to know anyone who was anyone within IRA circles in Belfast. I effected a reintroduction to my old friend from Eurodisney, Joe 'The Hawk' Haughey. Getting to know men of this pedigree was one thing; earning their complete trust was another matter entirely.

By now, I had worked out an effective way of winning IRA men over: by involving them in moneymaking scams. Almost without exception, IRA men were skint. IRA 'staff' got thirty or forty quid a week to supplement their social security.

Volunteers got nothing at all. As such, even the most paranoid IRA volunteer was susceptible to a 'nixer'.

I dreamed up and put in place every scam imaginable, and invited IRA men to assist me. We smuggled in fireworks – prohibited in Northern Ireland – from the UK and sold them in the weeks leading up to Guy Fawkes. We adapted and subverted the latest developments in telecommunications to rip off phone companies. We smuggled alcohol and cigarettes. We moved dodgy electrical goods. We burned counterfeit CDs. Once I became a partner in crime with an IRA man, I inevitably became a partner in everything else too. Out of mutual benefit came mutual trust and a bond. I set about becoming indispensable to these men. If they needed something – anything – I got it for them. Mobile phones, used cars, security cameras – if you wanted it, I was the man to ask.

Away from the Belfast faces, I carried on my work with the IRA's explosives-development team. The success of the flashgun detonation device opened up a whole new world of destructive potential. We realised that the most mundane items of everyday life had the potential to detonate a bomb, and kill. Even the beep of a telephone answering machine had a frequency that could trigger a device.

The most terrifying new research, however, was into the use of infrared to detonate bombs. We discovered that photographic slave units existed that could be triggered by infrared, and this brought all sorts of advantages. When using a photographic flashgun to trigger a device, the button-man had to be about 100 yards from the slave unit. As such, the bomber was in the vicinity of the device and so at risk from flying shrapnel or the latest terrorist peril, CCTV. What's more, a flash from a photographic flashgun is clearly visible. A soldier could immediately detect where it came from, turn and open fire. However, an infrared beam – such as that which turns over the channels on your TV – isn't visible to the naked eye. It can carry much further than a flash, and there's no way of scrambling it. In effect, a terrorist could trigger a bomb from half a mile away by simply directing the infrared beam in the right direction. The security forces would have no way of obstructing the beam or working out where it was coming from.

The potential for mayhem boggled the minds of my handlers, who debriefed me constantly about the progress of the infrared research. My meetings with them were now altogether more elaborate affairs. Gone were the days when I would pull into a car park, bundle myself into the back of a van and get driven off somewhere. By now, my face was familiar to so many IRA people that there was a very real danger I would be spotted by someone anywhere in Northern Ireland, or in southern Ireland for that matter. I had been to the mainland for occasional debriefings in the past, but now the decision was taken to fly me to London regularly. For each visit I would be given a reference number for a flight from Aldergrove Airport to Heathrow, and a pseudonym. My contact at the other end would be holding a card bearing this pseudonym. I would be driven to a hotel somewhere in central London – the Grosvenor in Victoria, another plush hotel in the Strand – checked in and told to attend a certain conference room at a certain time. As when I had been in London to discuss the flashgun development with my handlers, the conference rooms were invariably booked under a company name. It was no longer a good old natter over tea and biscuits. These days our meetings took the form of fully fledged debriefings lasting two days, sometimes three. They were painfully intense. Over and over again, I would be asked to go through every last tiny morsel of information in microscopic detail. Each titbit was devoured word by word, as if it was a new commandment from the Lord. I soon recognised the benefits of their devotion to detail.

Now that I was hanging about with the Belfast boys, I was picking up bits of intelligence about planned operations. Piecing together my titbits of information with other intelligence, my handlers were able to prevent countless IRA operations, both major and minor. Because of the way the intelligence was gathered, the Provos were never able to pinpoint exactly where the leak must have come from – at least, they didn't seem to suspect me.

As far as they were concerned, I was travelling to and from London to work. To ensure the ruse stood up to any checks by the IRA, I was registered with an employment agency near Victoria station. Travelling to work on the mainland was not unusual – work was so scarce in the North that thousands made the journey for work every week. Soon, however, I was making a far more glamorous journey. In 1993, on behalf of the Provisional IRA, I was sent to the United States.

I was told to recruit three suitable people to travel with me to the States and participate in the latest Republican fundraising wheeze. Once again, I told my handlers all about it. Three of our team would take a cab in New York. The fourth member would be waiting in a hire car. As soon as the driver of the hire car felt it was appropriate, he would smack good and hard into the back of the yellow taxi containing his three pals.

The three taxi passengers would prove to have very tender necks. Needless to say, the connection between the three whiplashed, dazed and mentally traumatised taxi passengers and the driver of the hire car would not be made known. At the first opportunity, the three accident victims would contact a well-known and particularly aggressive firm of New York personal-injury lawyers. The compensation – often six- or seven-figure sums – would be carved up between the participants of the scam and the Provisional IRA. This ruse made the IRA many millions.

However, setting up a fake car crash wasn't the sole purpose of my trip to New York. Only two outlets in the UK sold the infrared slave units, and one was in Belfast. If we purchased a slave unit from either of these stores, it could be easily traced. From an IRA perspective, there was a risk that the security forces had placed both stores on alert to let them know if any purchase took place. Alternatively, the outlets could have been told by the security services to sell an infrared slave unit only in the event of the purchaser supplying full identification and paying by credit card.

Someone in MI5 did their homework and discovered a store in New York that sold exactly the type of infrared slave unit that we required. I told senior IRA figures in Belfast about the New York store. Days later, I was handed £2,000 to travel to New York and buy two models.

When I told Bob and Pete about my proposed trip to New York, they recognised the opportunities straight away. That the infrared threat was being taken seriously was confirmed at our next meeting when Bob and Pete announced that they would be making the trip to New York as well, along with a man from RUC Special Branch.

I was handed a US mobile phone number. It would be Bob's number in New York. All I had to do was purchase the component part, ring Bob and meet him and Pete at a secret location in New York. However, my work for them in the Big Apple wouldn't end there. They wanted me to help them find someone in New York – someone whom I had once known extremely well.

The man I have been referring to as Johnny was my fellow bomb-making graduate. A year earlier, a senior Provo in South Armagh handed me four small photographs of him and told me to get him a fake passport in a hurry. He told me Johnny wanted to start a new life in New York with his common-law wife and young daughter. However, because of convictions for possession of explosives and assaulting a policeman, he wouldn't be granted an entry visa to the Land of the Free. I didn't ask why it needed to be done in a hurry. With the full backing of my handlers, I produced a fake passport within three days. It bore Johnny's picture and the name of my unwitting and totally innocent brother-in-law.

I assumed that our ruse had worked and that he had made it into the US, as I hadn't seen him or heard from him since.

The trouble was, nor had the FBI – and it had been tasked with keeping tabs on Johnny. They photographed him for a few weeks but then lost him. Now they were desperate to locate him again, though they didn't say why. Would I be able to help?

I assumed that, to warrant such attention from the FBI, Johnny had been implicated in something very serious. I decided to play along with the sting. I rang his father in Kilkeel and told him I was heading to New York for a short break. Could I meet up with Johnny?

'Of course,' said the poor father, 'he'd be delighted to see you. He's so grateful for what you did for him.'

'Oh, it was nothing,' I said.

'Ring me when you're over there and I'll get in touch with him then,' said the father cryptically. 'He'll meet you somewhere for a drink or a bite to eat.'

'Great,' I said, but I felt sly and sneaky. I snapped out of it quickly though. I reminded myself that, even though I liked Johnny as a person, he was an IRA bomb-maker. He deserved what was coming to him.

It was the day after St Patrick's Day when we flew into Newark Airport. My handlers had already been there a few days. I envied them their lives. New York was covered in fresh snow and felt magical. Then I remembered all the cynical exercises I had to complete during my two-day stay, and those magical feelings dissipated like the vapour from my mouth. There was to be no time for sightseeing, that was for sure.

Snow proved the perfect backdrop to a slapstick road crash. My tender-necked associates acted their little hearts out. One of the 'victims' got out of the taxi and genuinely slipped heavily on the snow, spraining his left arm. The others had to work very hard not to laugh.

I checked into my hotel, a low-grade dump. My room was on the twelfth floor but there was no view. Cramped and stifling hot, the view was a stretch of grey wall four feet from the glass. I rang Johnny's father. I told him where I was staying and said I would love to meet Johnny the following night as I was flying back to Ireland the next day. His father said I would be hearing from one of them.

The following morning, I headed to the specialist store to purchase the infrared remote system. To my horror, the shop was closed for a Jewish holiday. I knocked and knocked and knocked but nobody emerged. I couldn't believe it. I had no back-up plan, no alternative store lined up just in case. I rang Bob.

He laughed, which was a relief. He told me to come to their hotel just off Times Square to discuss the plan for Johnny. I arrived in a plush and vast reception area to find my four handlers sitting in leather couches. A man was playing 'The Good Life' on piano. Fucking right, I thought to myself.

'Jesus, you want to see the dump I'm staying in,' I said when I got close.

They didn't seem remotely embarrassed.

'Jewish holiday!' I said. 'Can you believe it?'

They didn't seem overly concerned.

'Doesn't matter,' said Bob.

They didn't appear at all worried. Bob changed the subject

to Johnny. I was to invite him to dinner at a grill on 43rd Street. The table had been booked. All I had to do was get him there. They would do the rest.

'You're not planning on charging in and arresting him, are you?' I asked. I didn't want it to look like I had set him up. Word would get back.

'We want to find out where he lives,' said Bob, 'that's all.'

When I got back to New York's worst hotel, the slouching receptionist told me that Johnny had called and left a number. I went up to my room, switched on the TV and rang him. The news was all about Northern Ireland. Gerry Adams was holding secret meetings with John Hume, the leader of the SDLP. Commentators speculated as to whether they were drawing up a plan for peace. Johnny answered the phone. He sounded genuinely pleased to hear from me. Of course he would come to dinner, as long as he could pay. It was the least he could do.

I got there first and waited at the bar. I inspected every wall and corner. Nothing looked remotely untoward.

'Kevin!' Johnny's voice startled me. We shook hands. I could tell he fancied a beer. I thought I had better get him down to our table. I assumed we were being bugged or filmed. If he got comfortable at the bar, there was every chance we would end up sat there all night. After the day I'd had, I wasn't prepared to take any chances.

'Let's eat,' I said, and led the way.

We sat down. He sipped beer and told me excitedly about his new job as a carpenter, his flat in Queens and his new role training a Gaelic football team. He looked years younger than the haunted man I last saw back home. I told him as much and he said he was 'glad to be away from it'.

I was flabbergasted by his openness and lack of suspicion. He didn't even ask me why I was in New York. Had he given up his IRA career completely? I decided to find out. We tucked into a pair of pan-sized steaks, which must have weighed a pound each. While we washed them down with a few beers, I told Johnny why I was in New York.

His eyes lit up at the barbaric possibilities of infrared. Once a bomb-maker, I thought to myself ...

I took out the £2,000. 'Could you buy the stuff and send it back?' I asked.

'No problem,' said Johnny, but declined to take the cash.

We left the grill laughing at some old tale or other. We shook hands and assured each other that we would stay in touch, which we knew we wouldn't. I turned away and set off for my hotel. The snow looked brown and scoured. Steam rose like ghosts from the pavement vents. Maybe Johnny was genuinely trying to make a fresh start, a clean break from the Provisional IRA and the Troubles. Now, thanks to me, he wasn't quite out of the woods yet. By purchasing the infrared systems and sending them back to Northern Ireland, he was still aiding and abetting the war.

A few months later, I found out the fruits of my duplicity with Johnny. He was tapped by the FBI to become an informant. A man approached him in a bar and introduced himself as an FBI agent. He flashed his badge and told Johnny he would be getting a visit from Immigration and Naturalisation Service (INS) officials next week.

Johnny knew that his illegal status in the US had been rumbled. In a state of panic – and desperate to escape – he left and walked into the next bar he saw. The agent followed him in. He told Johnny he was willing to strike a deal. If he co-operated with the FBI, arrangements could be made to secure his residential status in the US. The FBI wanted him to spy on pro-IRA activists in the Irish-American community and to report back. Johnny told him to fuck off.

On leaving the bar, Johnny was arrested by three INS agents. He spent several weeks in custody. Eventually, he was sent back to his old life in the Republic of Ireland. During my steak dinner with him, I couldn't tell for sure whether or not he was really trying to make a fresh start away from the Provisional IRA. If he was, then maybe the Provos would have let him walk away. One thing was for certain, the other side wasn't going to let him walk away from the war just like that. The intelligence services – those full-time professionals whose business is war – wanted their pound of flesh. I couldn't understand their thinking. Was it not enough for them that an IRA man was walking away from the war? Not for the first time, I found myself baffled by the motives of the intelligence services. It was clear to me that they weren't interested in peace in Northern Ireland – they wanted to win the war.

There were elements within the Provisional IRA that still wanted to win the war too. While the Hume–Adams initiative was gaining momentum, elements within the IRA were actively plotting to bring mayhem to the mainland.

In February, three bombs exploded at a gasworks in

Warrington, Lancashire. As one senior IRA man told me, this attack got more publicity and political attention than if three people had been blown up in Northern Ireland.

Almost a month later, on 20 March, a bomb planted in a bin in Warrington killed three-year-old Jonathan Ball and twelve-year-old Tim Parry. More than fifty people were injured, some seriously. According to the security services, the IRA had given 'an inadequate warning'. Within the IRA, the common myth peddled again and again was that warnings were cynically ignored by the security services to ensure more casualties and, as such, generate more adverse publicity for the Provisional IRA. I didn't buy that for one second.

A month after that, on 23 April 1993, a bomb ripped through the City of London, the capital's financial centre, killing one person and injuring thirty more.

Two IRA men who I cannot identify but will give the names Liam and Jimmy believed that the campaign on the mainland was finally getting the Provisional IRA the attention it deserved. Furthermore, with all these rumours of peace initiatives, attacks on the mainland were timely reminders that Sinn Fein's election manifesto promised the ballot box *and* the bullet.

'You're back and forward to England a lot,' said Jimmy to me one day. We were sitting with Liam in Jimmy's home.

'Aye,' I said, 'every few weeks.'

'We're keen to keep the momentum going there now,' said Jimmy. 'It's only when your average *Sun*-reader starts to worry about bombs going off in his back garden that you really start putting pressure on the Brits.'

He had a point there. 'I suppose you have some operations in mind,' I ventured.

'Major public events are the way forward,' said Jimmy.

Liam nodded enthusiastically.

'What sort of thing?' I said.

'The Grand National, for one,' said Jimmy.

'And Wembley Stadium,' added Liam. 'We had a good scout there. There's a long concrete walkway up to the stadium, the Wembley way. You've seen it on the telly, a massive walkway. It's the only way in and the only way out. Jesus, they'd be like sitting ducks.'

'There's the ring of steel in the City now,' said Jimmy, 'but Canary Wharf's an attractive proposition. Stuck out there in the middle of nowhere. Packed full of workers. That's another place we're having a good look at.'

I nodded thoughtfully. 'So,' I said, 'what do you want me to do?'

'We want you to sink a couple of arms dumps over there,' said Jimmy. 'You think you're up for it?'

'Yeah, of course,' I said.

'London's going to be our main target,' said Jimmy, 'but it's a bit easier in the North of England. We've had some good results there.'

I waited.

'We need a dump on the outskirts of London,' he said, 'and another one in Scotland. You're back and forward to London all the time. Sink one somewhere on the outskirts that you can get to easily. As far as Scotland goes, you can get over and back there on the ferry handy enough, or fly to Glasgow.

Sink one somewhere outside Glasgow, somewhere you can pick stuff up on your way down to England. Think you can do that?'

'Yeah,' I said, 'I'll start booking something up.'

'You know the rules about arms dumps, Kevin,' said Jimmy sternly. 'You sink them, then you're the only person who knows where they are, you understand? You're the only one who can gain access to them.'

That's what scared me about England. Operations on the mainland are so tight. When people start getting caught in England, it really does cause problems. If it goes wrong, only a few people have been involved, so the spotlight lands on each one of you. In Northern Ireland, there were loads of informants and loads of people connected to an operation. You could never pinpoint the tout – or at least it was very difficult to prove.

For a double agent, England is your last job. I didn't like it. I knew my time was coming near.

Of course, my handlers didn't share my concerns about safety. They were elated at this latest march forward in my IRA career. Bob said this represented my best chance yet of stopping a major atrocity.

'You stop an atrocity on the mainland,' said Bob, 'and we all look good.'

At our next meeting, they had it all planned out. They had sourced two specific areas where they wanted me to sink the dumps. They would meet me over there and help me sink them. They had even booked my flights and accommodation for the trip.

Jimmy handed me £1,500 for the mission. I flew to Prestwick Airport, a good twenty miles outside Glasgow, and spent the night in a Holiday Inn. The next morning, I was met in the hotel reception by Bob from MI5, Pete from the military and a man called George from Special Branch. I told Bob to drive me to a DIY store. The others followed in a second car. I had sunk several arms dumps in the Republic before, so I knew exactly what I needed. I bought a large cool box, rubber seals, heavy plastic covering, a spade, a pair of wellington boots and a roll of black bin-liners. The women on the tills didn't bat an eyelid as three men in smart suits helped me wheel my shopping out of the store.

We took the A77 towards Stranraer, then the A714 inland. Wooded mountains loomed high to my left. I kept my eyes peeled for landmarks, making a list of distances and turnings in a notebook.

We took a temporary road into dense wood, drove slowly for about four minutes, then got out. Experience taught me that an arms dump needed to be well away from the roadside, but there was no point trying to sink it in dense forest as everywhere looked exactly the same. Besides, these were commercial trees that could be mown down at any time. If the trees went, then so did my reference points. Worse than that, heavy machinery might uncover the arms dump.

'Can we drive on a bit?' I asked.

'Yeah,' said Bob, 'it's up to you now where you sink it.'

We came to a nature reserve. This was more like it. The

sign announcing the reserve was fixed and an ideal reference point. I checked a compass and headed due west into less dense deciduous forest. About half a mile in, I marked a spot in between three very distinctive trees. I measured the spot from each of these trees.

The car was driven up to the edge of the woods and I set to work. While I lugged the equipment into the forest, Pete filmed me and Bob took photographs. When I started to dig, they just stood around, smoking and joking. I should have bought more spades, I thought to myself.

It took me three hours to dig the hole. Tree roots made it a real struggle. All the soil had to be shovelled into a black bin-liner and spread out somewhere else. You didn't want park rangers wondering why someone had dug a large hole. At least my handlers had the decency to hold the bags open for me while I filled them with soil. However, they made it clear they didn't want to get dirty, so I had to haul the bags into the woods and empty them myself.

The plastic sheet which covered the dump was just five or six inches underground. Using my hands, I buried the spade last. If, by some amazing quirk of fate, the trees were felled or knocked down by a hurricane, the spade would be my insurance. I would be able to locate it with a metal detector. I carried the bin-liners back to the car, threw them in the boot and threw myself wearily into the back seat. I felt knackered.

'What's next?' I groaned.

'We're back to Prestwick,' said Bob. 'We're all flying down to Stansted this evening. We'll get you something to eat at the airport.'

For once, I wasn't stopped at the airport, but as usual I stayed in a different hotel to my handlers. As I lay on my single bed, surveying a curious stain on the ceiling, I pictured them clasping brandy tumblers in the foyer of some plush hotel up the road. I was a lowly private and they were the officers. I was growing a little tired of this.

My mobile phone rang and made me start. It was Jimmy wanting to know how it had gone.

'Well I'm not in prison, am I?' I joked.

He said he would ring again the following afternoon. He made it clear that the news he really wanted to hear was that I had successfully sunk a dump near London. I sensed this had proven a real challenge in the past.

The next morning, Bob drove me to another store and we repeated the exercise. We took the M11 to Harlow, and stopped at a Little Chef just outside the town. After breakfast, we strolled back to the car park.

'This place looks as good as any to me,' said Bob.

We walked to the back of the car park, through a little play area into some woods. A public bridleway carried on up through the trees. I followed it until I was out of sight from the car park. I could still hear the traffic on the M11 thundering past. This was ideal.

I made my way back down the hill and insisted they each carry something up with them. I measured a spot off a public-footpath sign into the woods and turned right into the woodland. I tramped over fallen twigs and undergrowth until I came to a circular dip between three trees, one of which was lying down almost horizontally. Three hours later, we emerged, me filthy, the other three spotlessly clean. God knows what people who saw us emerging from the woods must have thought.

'Right, that's that then,' I said to Bob.

'Not quite,' said Bob. 'We need you for another forty-eight hours. We need a full debrief about the arms dumps.'

I turned on my mobile phone. There were two missed calls, both from Jimmy.

'I told Jimmy I was flying back tonight,' I explained. 'How the fuck am I going to explain away two extra days?'

'Say you got some work or something,' said Bob.

'You don't understand,' I said. 'I gave him my full itinerary for the trip. They get very jumpy about changes of plan. I'll have to ring him and tell him something.'

'Turn your phone off,' said Bob, 'until we think of something. But you're coming to this debrief whether you like it or not.'

We stopped off at some services so that I could clean up. I wondered how many more times Jimmy failed to get through to me. What must he be thinking? My excuse for disappearing had better be a good one, otherwise I might be digging a third hole in the woods – for myself.

We got back in the car and headed into central London, Bob and Pete in pursuit. Bob explained that a conference room in a West End hotel had been booked for the next two days for my debriefing. When we pulled up outside, I asked Bob what I should do about Jimmy. He was expecting a phone call tonight and a meeting tomorrow.

'Whatever you do, don't ring him,' said Bob. 'I don't want

you to fuck things up. Leave it to me. I'll think of something.'

The debriefing was as intense as always. It became very clear very quickly that a bombing threat on the mainland was taken much more seriously than any planned operation in Northern Ireland. We went through every single detail again and again. I kept being told the same thing, over and over: 'Make sure no one else in the IRA finds out where these dumps are. You've got to be solely in charge of them.'

That evening, Bob told me he had worked out a way of deflecting Jimmy's suspicions.

'Say that, when you went to board your plane at Heathrow, you were arrested,' said Bob, 'and carted off to Paddington Green police station where you were held for forty-eight hours.' Paddington Green police station is where high-risk terror suspects are held.

I wondered aloud if Jimmy would buy it.

'Tomorrow night, we'll put you up in a hotel in Heathrow. Ring him from there and tell him what happened. We'll see if he swallows it.'

'He'd better,' I said.

'We'll run through your story tomorrow. Make sure you can give him some details about Paddington Green that only someone who had been there could know.'

I still wasn't satisfied.

'If Jimmy starts asking awkward questions,' said Bob, 'tell him to get a solicitor to check the custody records, which they're perfectly entitled to do.'

'Oh,' I said, 'and what will that prove?'

'I've got someone putting your name in the Paddington Green custody book right now,' said Bob. 'That's all the proof you'll ever need.'

We ran through my story again and again the next day. That night I rang Jimmy from my hotel bedroom in Heathrow. My handlers had a special attachment device which allowed them to listen in to the conversation.

'Where the fuck have you been?' was Jimmy's opening gambit.

'You won't fucking believe it,' I started, and off I went, telling him the entire fictional story in graphic and vivid detail. By now, I almost believed it myself.

He sounded dubious, so I hit him with my biggest shot.

'Get a solicitor to check the custody records if you don't believe me,' I said. 'I fucking stood there and watched them write my name in.'

That appeased him no end. When I met Jimmy the next day, he greeted me like a conquering hero. Of course, he wanted to hear all about it, but I could tell he was no longer suspicious. I handed him his change and launched into my tale one more time. This was becoming easy.

Jimmy told me that I might have to return to my dumps very soon. A package of Semtex and some Kalashnikovs were on their way to the UK. Was I around the following week if I needed to go back to England?

'Of course,' I said.

'Maybe it would be better if we put someone else in charge of them,' said Jimmy. 'Now that they've pulled you into Paddington Green, they'll be waiting for you next time.'

'No, no,' I said, 'leave it with me. Where I put these dumps, no one could follow me.'

It was the autumn of 1993. Over the following weeks, John Hume and Gerry Adams made two joint statements and announced the completion of the Hume–Adams initiative for peace. The British and Irish governments confirmed that they were holding secret talks with Sinn Fein, aimed at bringing about a cessation of the Provisional IRA's military campaign.

Like a glutton confronted with the threat of a diet, Northern Ireland's paramilitary organisations launched into an orgy of killing. On 23 October, a Provisional IRA bomb in a fish shop on Belfast's Protestant Shankill Road exploded prematurely, killing a bomber and nine innocent Protestants. A week later, on 30 October, the Loyalist Ulster Freedom Fighters opened fire on drinkers in the Rising Sun bar in Greysteel, County Derry, shooting dead six Catholics and one Protestant. One of the gunmen was heard to utter the words 'trick or treat' before unloading machine-gun fire on a pub full of innocent drinkers.

The British and Irish governments ploughed on regardless. On 23 December 1993, John Major and Albert Reynolds, the Irish Taoiseach, issued a joint declaration which became known as the Downing Street Declaration. It was a road map to peace.

Over Christmas, everyone on TV and radio talked about the 'Peace Dividend'. I figured that I possessed one of the biggest dividends of all. If peace broke out – and it seemed inevitable now – my work as a double agent would be complete. I could look forward to a pay-off. I had been told that I had the best part of £200,000 in my secret bank account for work completed on behalf of the British government. I dreamed of a new life away from Northern Ireland, away from suspicion and death. Surely, it was only a matter of time before I got my just desserts.

CHAPTER TEN

On 29 January 1994, Gerry Adams was granted a visa to enter the US by Bill Clinton. His rehabilitation from terrorist to international statesman was complete.

Less than a fortnight later, I put his cousin in prison.

In January 1994, Jimmy asked me to get hold of a 'basher' for him. A basher is a cloned mobile phone – the bill for the calls goes somewhere else, such as a large company, so the person using it can't be identified.

My handlers told me to go ahead and get one for Jimmy, but with one proviso. They wanted me to give it to them first, just for a couple of days. I didn't ask why, but it was fairly obvious. They planned to bug the phone, or insert some sort of tracking device.

I tried all my usual sources, but to no avail. When a week passed by, my handlers became worried that Jimmy would source a basher from someone else, thereby spoiling their plans. They told me to do whatever I had to do to get a phone, and to bring it to them first.

I saw no option but to go to a friendly mobile-phone shop and buy a new model. I bought the phone in my wife's name. She was totally unaware of the fact, but my handlers knew. I told them as much when I handed them the phone later that day. Two days later, I presented it to Jimmy. It really didn't seem much of a big deal.

A few days later, Jimmy got on to me again. The previous night, an IRA unit had been moving some gear when it crashed a car. Could I find him a replacement car? I said I would see what I could do. Again, I contacted my handlers. They told me to go ahead and buy a car for Jimmy, but to make sure to tell them the make, colour, the registration number and the time and place of delivery. Again, this was run-of-the-mill activity.

I bought the car from a second-hand-car dealer in Belfast for cash. He knew me as an IRA man from previous dealings, and always offered an excellent deal. I delivered the car to Jimmy.

Two days later, I was to go and see Jimmy at his home just off the Antrim Road, near the Waterworks park. When I turned into his street, I could see police officers and soldiers swarming all over the place. It was clear Jimmy's home was being raided. I drove past. I rang my handlers and told them I thought Jimmy had been arrested. They told me to sit tight. They would find out what was going on and ring me back.

At about half past eleven that morning they called me back. They said they wanted to meet me immediately. We picked a rendezvous point in a quiet car park around the back of a hospital. I got there first and waited. A Toyota van pulled up. I waited for the all-clear to approach. I got the signal and walked over to the van. I slid open the side door and got in. We drove to a safe house. Bob and Pete were waiting for me there. They told me to sit down. Then they told me what had happened ...

In the early hours of that morning, 10 February 1994, the RUC had intercepted an IRA unit in the Belmont area of east Belfast. The unit was on its way to murder a senior RUC man called Derek Martindale. Next came the bad news.

The mobile phone used on the job was the one I had supplied. The getaway car was also the one I had supplied. My handlers told me not to worry. They had it all under control. They then told me that my wife had been arrested an hour earlier. My home was being raided as we spoke. The RUC wanted to arrest me too.

My handlers told me to stay at the safe house for the day while they sorted things out. They would make some calls. The following day, I would have to be arrested too, otherwise my disappearance might look suspicious. Later that day, I was briefed about what would happen once I was under arrest. I would be taken to a Belfast holding centre. I was told to say nothing to the police, as they had no idea that I was an agent. My handlers said they would keep a close eye on everything that was going on. They would have the inside track.

The next morning, I returned home. Hours later, I was arrested by the RUC.

'You're going to Castlereagh,' said one officer, referring to the interrogation centre in Belfast, notorious to all Nationalists for its brutality.

I was driven there in a police car.

Once there, I was taken by two police officers down a long grey corridor into a gloomy interview room. The air was heavy with stale cigarette smoke and sweat. I sat down and waited.

In a matter of minutes, two detectives walked in. They sat down opposite me. One looked at his paperwork. The other one looked up at me and smiled. 'Who the fuck do you work for?' he said, sneering.

I didn't have to feign the look of surprise.

'Who the fuck do you work for?'

This time I stayed stony faced. I stared at a spot on the wall, over his shoulder.

The other cop looked up from his papers and spoke up for the first time. 'We need to know who you're working for,' he said in a softer voice, 'because it is all pointing at you.'

I said nothing.

'Come on, Kevin,' said the first officer, 'you set the whole team up. We couldn't have done it better ourselves.' Next thing, he started to sing. I recognised the tune immediately, 'There May be Trouble Ahead.'

I sat there, emotionless. Part of me desperately wanted to speak, to tell them that my wife knew nothing, and played no part in it. However, I knew that to talk would be a disaster.

There is an IRA expression: 'Silent for seven days or porridge for seven years.' At best, I would talk myself into the conspiracy to kill Martindale and face a lengthy spell in prison. At worst, I would reveal myself as a double agent. How long before that hot snippet of news leaked out? I would be down a hole in a matter of days.

'To be honest, Kevin,' said the second cop, 'we're not going to bother asking you any more questions.' He took his papers up in his hands, bounced them a couple of times on the desk like a newsreader at the end of a bulletin, smiled at me and then stood up. 'What's the point? We know you're working for us, one of our agencies, as a grass or a mole. We know. And, if we can work it out, so can the Provos.'

With that, his colleague mockingly performed another rendition of 'There May be Trouble Ahead'.

The air in my lungs emptied all at once. That knot in my stomach was back. It did all point to me. I supplied the mobile phone and the car for a major IRA operation. While the unit is on its way to carry out this operation, the RUC suddenly appears out of nowhere. Clearly the IRA would realise it had a mole, an informant, a 'tout' on the inside. As the newest face, and the man who supplied vital equipment, I'd be in the spotlight. How the hell was I going to get out of this one?

The officers were as good as their word. They didn't question me again that day. Or the next, or the next. I was left to stew. All I could do was worry myself sick about what might happen next. I felt fear now. Real fear. Fear for my life and for the safety of my wife. I hadn't been able to speak to her since she had been arrested. What must she be going through?

'At least she knows nothing,' I told myself over and over again, 'at least she knows nothing.'

Finally, after four nights in Castlereagh, I was released. My wife was let out at the same time. My heart sank as I watched her emerge dazed and pale from the gates of this fierce and intimidating building. It was like watching her emerge from the mouth of a monster. I felt sick with myself. This was all down to me. I had put her through this ordeal. We hugged. She felt frail in my arms.

I decided there and then that my handlers had to pull me out this time. As soon as I got home, I rang them. I was desperate for reassurance.

'You're all right,' said Pete, 'we've got the inside track on it. You're not the prime suspect at all. You'll be fine.'

'But it all points to me,' I said. 'The phone, the car – it can only be me.'

'No, listen,' said Pete, 'how many times have we been in this situation? Have we ever made a bad call before? Anyone connected to that op could have talked, Kevin, and you know it. The man who sold you the car might be a tout. The man who sold you the phone might be a tout. They can't prove a thing.'

These words provided relief. In a way, Pete was right. It would be hard for the IRA to prove that the leak came from me. If I didn't confess to anything, I would probably be OK. Despite this, I still felt fear. I knew the call would come from the IRA. I knew I would end up being quizzed for hour after hour in a darkened room. I knew that one slip would be potentially lethal. Dread hung on my every thought and action.

Of course, I couldn't tell my wife the truth. In fact, I told her nothing at all. I said it was all a misunderstanding. I followed a procedure that I had followed for so long now I did it instinctively. I told her not to ask me to tell her anything, and I told her nothing. If it all went horribly wrong, her complete ignorance would be her salvation.

I didn't sleep that night. I kept running everything through my mind, again and again, over and over. Would I be OK? Should I believe the handlers? What if the IRA found proof? Would they kill me even if they didn't have the proof? All it took was for three judges – each one far from independent – to decide I was a tout, and that would be that. They would probably play with my balls for a few days first, find out all they could. Then I would be found dead in a ditch.

Morning, the only respite to a sleepless night, arrived like judgement day. The sound of the front-door bell made my heart sink to the floor. It was the brother of an OC whom I had helped put away three years earlier. 'Well?' I said. 'What can I do for you?'

'You've to go up to Belfast straight away. Security unit want to have a chat with you.'

'No problem,' I said, leaning against the door all casual.

'You've to bring your wife too,' he said.

'Ach, she knows nothing about anything,' I said.

'Bring her too,' he said, 'or we'll get a team and fucking drag her to Belfast. Understood?'

'Right,' I said. 'And where are we to go exactly?'

'Go to Unity Flats, they're expecting you at two o'clock.'

I told my wife the news. She visibly trembled.

'We've nothing to worry about,' I said as convincingly as I could. 'Nothing whatsoever. You'll see.'

I really wanted to convince her that everything would be OK. She managed a faint smile, but I knew that she knew something was seriously wrong, that I was in deep trouble. At least I knew she would stay strong. I knew she would stick by me no matter what. I knew she would be astute enough not to get hysterical, and not to demand answers. She understood how things worked.

I drove to a familiar phone box and called my handlers.

'They won't be able to prove anything,' said Bob. 'Just tell them you did what you were told by the IRA. You knew nothing about the Martindale operation, and you've no idea what's going on. OK?'

'Yeah, Bob,' I said, 'I know the drill. I'm just not sure it's going to wash. What if they've already made up their minds?'

'If they'd plans for you, Kevin,' said Bob, 'they wouldn't have told you to bring your wife along, would they?'

This was true. I started feeling a little better.

'Don't start thinking like that, Kevin,' said Bob. 'You've got to stay strong here. You've got to brazen it out. You've been through worse than this and come out the other side.'

My brain seized on the 'you' in Bob's last statement: 'You've been through worse than this and come out the other side.' Bob and Pete had always spoken about what 'we've' been through: 'We've been through worse than this before.' It always used to irritate me. Now suddenly he had reverted to using 'you'. Was I on my own now? Did he know something?

I dismissed this as paranoia. I decided to dwell instead on all the close scrapes that I had survived in the past. As we drove up to Belfast in silence, I thought about all my narrow escapes. There was the incident in Dundalk when I was ordered to get on my knees and say an act of contrition. There was the time we pulled straws to decide who would execute a tout. There was the time I narrowly prevented two IRA men opening fire on a British army patrol.

Bob was right. I just had to brazen it out. The IRA could prove nothing.

I rang the doorbell to Liam's flat. He came out.

'How are you, Kevin?' he said, shaking my hand warmly. 'And this must be your wife.'

He showed us inside the door of his flat, then set about looking for his jacket and his keys. You would think we were away to the park for an afternoon stroll. Finally, he led us out the door, along a drab concrete walkway, up a flight of concrete steps and along another walkway until we arrived at a red front door. It wasn't locked.

Inside, the IRA's premier arbiter of truth, the man we know only as Michael, was sitting on the stairs. He led my wife into one room. I was led by Liam into another. It was a mirror image of the home I had prepared in Omeath for an interrogation. As in the other home, a lone chair faced a bare wall. I was invited to sit down. Suddenly, I heard a door opening and feet scuffing the floor.

'Well, Kevin,' came the voice. It was Michael. I gulped

hard. 'You do realise that you're now to be de-briefed by the IRA security unit.'

'I do, yes,' I said, as firmly as I could. It was a relief to get those first words out. I breathed hard and told myself to stay strong and firm.

'You know who I am, yes?' said Michael.

'I do, yeah,' I said.

'OK. I want to ask you about the Martindale operation, all you know about it, any help you gave. Do you understand?'

I nodded.

'Right then, off you go,' he said.

I told him how Jimmy had asked me to get him a basher and a car. I explained how I got the phone in my wife's name without her knowing.

'She really had no part in this whatsoever,' I protested. 'She knows absolutely nothing.'

I said that acquiring a phone and a used car were my only functions in the operation. I didn't know anything about the operation itself. This part was easy. I was just telling the truth.

He moved on to my arrest and to my interrogation in Castlereagh.

'What did you say to the peelers?' said my interrogator.

'I didn't open my mouth,' I said.

'And what did they ask you?'

I didn't tell him what had actually taken place at Castlereagh – about how they didn't ask me any questions because they assumed that I was working for someone – and I regurgitated stories I had heard over the years about the tactics used by officers at Castlereagh.

'They kept telling me I was facing a murder rap,' I lied, 'and that my wife had started talking. Of course, I knew this was bullshit. My wife knows nothing about anything.'

This went on for hours. Finally, Michael said I could go home. 'But I want you back here in two days' time.'

'And my wife?' I asked.

'You can ask her yourself in a minute,' said Michael. With that, he left the room.

'There,' said Liam, 'that wasn't so bad, was it?'

I felt like telling him to fuck off.

My wife stood in the hallway. Her face was drawn and her eyes were red. When we got to the car, she started sobbing. She didn't have to tell me that she'd been ordered back as well. This was breaking my heart.

I pulled in at a lay-by and rang my handlers. I demanded a meeting the next day. They agreed.

The meeting was more of the same. 'We're watching,' said Bob. 'We'll know if things go wrong.'

I explained that I didn't really care about being hauled over the coals myself. What I couldn't stand was watching my wife suffer.

'It's not right,' I said. 'She's a total innocent, yet she's arrested by the police, then by the IRA.'

'It's good for your cover,' said Pete, 'you both being taken to Castlereagh. And they probably know by now that she knows nothing. They're making her come back to put pressure on you.'

'They can't prove a thing,' said Bob, as usual. 'I mean, had you been privy to the operation itself, that would be a different story. We'd have pulled you out by now.'

'And will you pull me out if this starts getting too heavy?' I said. 'As that was always the deal.'

'It won't come to that,' said Pete. 'Stick to your guns and you'll be fine.'

We returned to Unity Walk in Belfast two days later for our second 'debriefing'. We went through the motions with Liam and were led to the same flat as before. We were split up again, and taken into the same rooms. I didn't have to be asked to sit down. I was ready for this now. I'd had enough.

There was no blindfold. That was a relief. Perhaps I was already home and dry. Perhaps the second meeting was just a formality.

The door opened. Footsteps approached. I heard the record button being pressed down on the ancient tape recorder. The sound of the tape wheels grinding around were deafening. I hadn't noticed these the day before. Why were they taping it?

'OK, Kevin,' said the voice, 'let's run through the Martindale operation again. Everything you know and everything you did.'

It was a man named Martin. We had been introduced but I didn't really know him. I had a sudden realisation: Michael must be with my wife. If that fucker upset her, I'd pursue him to the ends of the earth.

I ran through my story again. It was even easier than before. I got a phone for Jimmy in my wife's name. Have I mentioned that she knows absolutely nothing? I got a car for Jimmy from a second-hand-car dealer known to the IRA.

Have I mentioned that my wife knows absolutely nothing about this either? That was all I knew.

I repeated my stories about Castlereagh, but I knew that the only thing that mattered as far as my interrogation was concerned was that I didn't talk. I could make anything else up – threats, brutality, assault. I didn't talk so I was in the clear.

'Right, I think we'll take a little breather there,' said Martin. 'We'll resume in five minutes. Michael wants to ask you about a few other Newry ops that went wrong.'

Martin left the room and the blood left my body. The tape recorder clunked off. I took a good lungful of tepid air and tried to stop my mind racing. What the fuck was going on? What had they got on me?

The wait was intolerable. Finally, the door opened and footsteps approached.

'We've spoken to everyone now,' said Michael, 'and it's all pointing to you.'

My heart was banging. My head was rattling. What was going on?

I felt a finger jab into the side of my face.

'I think you're a Brussel.' He spat the words into my face.

'No,' I said, the vigorous shake of my head shifting my chair closer to the wall.

'It all points to you,' he shouted, now on my other side. 'The phone, the car, everything is pointing to you.'

I knew that if I flinched I was dead. If I gave him a sign, he would seize on it. I couldn't show any signs of weakness. I couldn't give him an opening. I had seen it before. Next thing I would be in knots, jabbering away like an idiot, giving away all sorts of things. I had seen men withstand six, eight hours of this for two or three days – only to start talking suddenly. And, once they started, they couldn't stop. They talked themselves into their graves, as if it was almost cathartic. Don't let him in, I shouted inside my head, don't give him any signs. He can't prove a thing. My heart hammered away at my chest. I suddenly felt like heaving.

'You're going down a hole, Fulton!' Michael's voice was soft now, menacing, his breath tickled my left ear. 'Which road do you want to close?' he asked mockingly.

'I told you all I know,' I shouted. 'I knew fuck all about that operation. Fuck all. I got Jimmy the stuff he wanted, and that was that.'

I heard some paper being rustled. Christ, I thought, what now?

'You knew plenty about other operations that went tits up,' said Michael, 'didn't you, Fulton?'

I really needed to focus now, really concentrate. Like a batsman facing a fresh fast bowler, I had to dig in. I had to meet it face on, coolly and precisely.

'What about the mortar attack on the courthouse in Newry?' said Michael.

'That was looked into at the time,' I said. 'There wasn't a tout.'

'What about poor old Sean Mathers?'

'We found that tout there,' I said.

'Aye, but that tout didn't know about Jervis Marks's op,' said Michael. 'You did.'

Fuck, I thought, someone from Newry's been talking. Someone's been checking me out.

'There was a milkman who suddenly retired,' said Michael. 'You were involved in that, weren't you?'

'I was,' I said, 'but how the fuck was anyone to know he was going to retire?'

'And the cleaner you were supposed to whack,' said Michael, 'he retired too. Do you see what I'm getting at, Fulton? Your ops seemed to be dogged by misfortune.'

'Look,' I said, 'we've been unlucky with some things, but I've been involved in plenty of ops that went right too. I'm no fucking tout!'

'We'll be the judges of that,' said Michael. 'And the jury. And the fucking executioner. Do you understand?'

I had seen Michael in action before, switching from reasonable to homicidal in a flash, constantly wrong-footing a suspect. I had seen it but nothing could prepare you for it. I felt utterly disorientated. I felt vulnerable. I felt that, if this went on much longer, I would let something slip.

'And now Martindale as well,' roared Michael directly into my ear. 'You supply the phone, you supply the car, and suddenly an RUC unit materialises out of nowhere.'

He leaned in close now so that I could feel and smell his breath. 'And you're telling me you're not a tout.'

'I'm not a tout,' I said with real conviction, because I wasn't. It was an easy charge to deny. I wasn't some grass who had been turned by the other side. 'I'm no fucking tout,' I repeated.

'I want to see you again in forty-eight hours,' said Michael. With that, he left the room.

I sat there, shocked into inertia. It took me a full five minutes to pull myself together and get to my feet. Liam put his notes to the ground. 'Different venue next time,' he said, as if we were planning a game of cards. 'Artillery House. I'll get someone to fill you in on the details.'

'Great,' I said, as I limped out into the hallway. My wife looked like she needed a blood transfusion.

Without even a hint of self-consciousness, Liam shook our hands as if we'd just been round for tea and a slice of cake and let us out.

My legs felt wobbly on the concrete. I clutched her arm and held on to it like a drowning man. She felt as tense as a hair-coiled spring. The tears came, bitter this time. Each sob convulsed her entire frame. 'He threatened to shoot me,' she said.

'Who?' I asked. 'Michael?'

She nodded. The feeling that coursed through my body then scared me. At that moment, I could have happily murdered Michael in the most gruesome fashion imaginable. I felt blind hatred and murderous rage.

There was no way I was going back for another interrogation. I was for the high jump. Michael, the clever bastard, had figured it all out. He was to me. He had done his homework and he knew the truth. He wouldn't need proof. The fucker would whack me himself if he got half a chance.

I wanted out, and quickly. For thirteen years, I had played the role of IRA terrorist. Now the game was up. I had been hopelessly compromised by the Martindale affair. If I ever got compromised, I would be pulled out. That was the deal.

They owed me. A new home abroad. A new identity. My two hundred grand.

I pulled up in Dromore, walked into yet another phone box and rang my handlers. I eventually got through to Pete. 'I want out,' I said, 'and I fucking mean it this time.'

'What? What are you talking about?'

'You've got to pull me out, Pete,' I said. 'Michael is on to me.'

'What do you mean, he's on to you?' said Pete. 'Can he prove anything?'

'He's on to me. He literally listed the ops that I've compromised one by one,' I said. 'The fucker's going to get me whacked, one way or another.'

'I don't think you understand,' said Pete. 'We've got the very best information on this. The inside track. They suspect someone else. You're 100 per cent safe. He's pulling your wire.'

'You'll be pulling me dead out of a ditch if you don't do what I say,' I screamed down the phone. 'PULL ME OUT NOW!'

'You've got to go back there on Thursday,' said Pete. 'You've got to brazen it out. He's bluffing.'

'You weren't there,' I said. 'I'm telling you. He's already decided that I'm going down a hole. I'm a fucking dead man. You know the deal. I've been compromised. Now you've got to pull me out. That's the deal, Pete. That's the fucking deal.'

'It's not that easy,' said Pete.

'Dying isn't fucking easy, Pete,' I shouted.

'Look, let's meet tomorrow,' he said. 'We'll try and sort something out. But I can tell you now, you're in no danger.'

'Don't keep fucking saying that,' I screamed. 'I'm a dead man! I supplied the phone. I supplied the car. You've really fucked me. I want out. That was the deal, Pete,' I shouted. 'You owe me.'

Silence.

Finally, Pete spoke. He sounded like a teacher trying to explain something to a particularly thick pupil. 'They've got nothing concrete on you. Listen to me. They suspect someone else. You must go back on Thursday. I promise you, that will be the end of it.'

'Fucking right it'll be the end of it,' I shouted, smacking down the receiver. Suddenly, after 15 years, I was beginning to see the angles. I took three quick deep breaths. I had to be calm for my wife. I got into the car, gripped her right hand and told her everything was going to be all right.

That night I packed a bag, and the next morning I booked a flight to London. I told my wife I was going 'offside' for a while. As ever, she understood.

I decided to let things blow over. I was convinced that, in a week or two, my handlers would come to understand why I'd fled. I believed they'd quickly recognise that I'd been hopelessly compromised by the Martindale incident. I believed they'd pull me out and look after me. I truly believed this. This promise had sustained me for 15 years through countless near-death scrapes. Why would they lie to me? I'd done almost everything they'd ever asked. Bob and Pete were not just my handlers, they'd become my confidantes, my conscience, my friends. About a week later,

I decided that I had better call my handlers and let them know I was safe. I went into a phone box in Camden Town, North London, and rang my special number. The man who answered insisted that I had got through to a forklift company in Essex. I hung up and redialled. This time the man from the forklift company was less friendly.

I asked him if he was in any way connected to the security services.

'Are you fucking taking the piss?' he said.

'No really,' I said, 'I'm genuine.'

The phone went dead. I had a second number, but that was no longer in operation. I rang the operator to check that I didn't need a special code. But I had rung the right numbers. I decided that there must be some other explanation.

A week or so later, I rang Scotland Yard and explained my situation to someone. They were courteous but they couldn't help me. They told me I should ring the British army or the Home Office. Two dozen phone calls and more than fifty pounds in coins later, I was going around the bureaucratic loop for the third time. I realised it was useless.

Fuck it, I thought, and I rang the RUC in Newry. I asked to speak to one of three officers who had been my sworn enemies for many, many years. When I told him my story, he refused to believe it. I said I didn't care – I needed to speak with someone from Special Branch. Of course, Special Branch had no record of my handler, or of me.

Now finally, in a phone box in London, I could see the angles. I'd been compromised by Martindale. I could no longer function as a double agent. As such, I was no longer of any use to the security services. When the IRA investigated Martindale, my handlers tried to lull me into a false sense of security so that I'd go back to that third interrogation and get whacked. I was supposed to get executed so that my handlers – and British intelligence – wouldn't have to look after me.

My handlers counted on the IRA executing me. Now I was still alive, they'd resorted to plan B – cut me loose and deny ever knowing me. They could do this easily. It's not like I had an official employment record to produce. There was nowhere for me to turn.

I felt betrayed. However, I had underestimated British intelligence. It took many years, but eventually I discovered the full extent of their betrayal of me. My handlers didn't just want me dead to save money, they wanted the Provisional IRA to whack me for an altogether more dark, devious and – to me at least – shocking reason.

They wanted to sacrifice me to protect another double agent operating within the upper levels of the Provisional IRA. This secret agent had made it to a higher level within the IRA than I had and so – in the dog-eat-dog world of intelligence – he was worth preserving at my expense. Indeed, my execution would have significantly boosted this double agent's standing and power base within the IRA. To my horror, I discovered that this double agent was none other than Michael – my interrogator and tormentor-in-chief and the IRA internal security's most ruthless interrogator. Like me, he too was working for British intelligence. My handlers were setting up one British double agent, Michael, to expose and execute another one, me. Of course, this would have boosted Michael's cover and reputation within the IRA while I would have been found dead in a ditch. The news bulletins would report the discovery of my body as the execution of a known IRA man. They'd probably speculate as to the motive for the hit. They'd most likely opt for an internal feud or because I'd been suspected of informing. In short, I'd have been another anonymous victim of internal paramilitary 'housekeeping'.

My secret life would have died with me.

CHAPTER ELEVEN

15 August 1998. 3.09pm. A date and time seared on my memory. But not one of those John F Kennedy moments. I don't recall precisely what I was doing that sunny afternoon with the same far-removed enthusiasm that some people, as if participating in a mildly amusing national game, remember JFK's assassination.

I sometimes wish I could. Instead, every time I recall what I was doing that day – the day of the Omagh atrocity – my stomach tightens and I swallow hard. I remember the heart-quickening, blind panic. And I remember being seized by one thought: could I have done anything more to stop it?

I also try to summon up images of those poor families ripped apart by the atrocity, the worst of more than thirty years of carnage. How did they feel? What of their pain now? Perhaps I do this partly to reproach myself for only seeming to dwell on how *I* felt when I heard the news. The thoughts compete inside my head. But, if I am honest, it is the selfish thoughts that always win; they are the ones that rise to the surface first. I put this down to human nature. Besides, how could anyone who hasn't experienced it begin really to understand that depth of grief. Twenty-nine people were massacred that day in the most monstrous way. Blown to pieces while out shopping. Men, women and children. Catholics and Protestants.

I was in Tenerife when I heard. I had flown there the day before on a family holiday. Two days before that, I had met a senior IRA figure. It was to prove a fateful, life-changing encounter, although it didn't seem so at the time. I suppose they never do. At the time, he was a senior figure in the Real IRA. The Reals. The dissident Republicans who couldn't stomach the Good Friday Agreement. As for myself, I was no longer the British army's 'brave' double agent. Shunned by the IRA over the Martindale fiasco, dropped like a brick by my handlers who obviously thought I had become a liability, I was now operating, or rather scratching around, in a world where the distinctions between right and wrong, the good and the bad guys, were as blurred as ever.

I had left the IRA and become a peripheral figure, floating around under the umbrella of the Republican movement, doing insignificant jobs for the cause. I was someone viewed with suspicion for whom there was no real place; tolerated, at best.

I had escaped execution over Martindale because Michael and the boys hadn't managed to secure a confession. Nor did they have any proof, and they needed one or the other. Some may find it surprising, but the IRA is rigidly strict about such matters.

So, with a question mark hanging over me, I was cast adrift in choppy waters, one of the outsiders, a man not to be trusted. As far as the IRA was concerned, it was a case of out of sight, out of mind. I was now drifting between England, the Far East and different addresses in Northern Ireland, never staying in one place too long. My options were distinctly limited. I couldn't have got a proper job even if I had wanted one. How could I? What would I have put on my CV? Try explaining my employment history to the man at Newry meat factory. I could picture the job interview. 'I have been an IRA double agent for the last thirteen years, but I've always known that my true destiny lies in packing pork chops ...'

Inevitably, I drifted back into the one field I knew about – the spying game. To begin with, it was low-level work, nothing like the heady excitement of the old days. I was feeding stuff to HM Customs, details of IRA smuggling operations – mostly drugs and arms – that I had picked up from the past. In fact, a lot of it was information I had given my handlers a long time ago but which they hadn't seemed interested in at the time.

Because of the nature of the stuff I was supplying – it became too heavy for Customs, I suppose – I was passed to C13, the RUC's anti-racketeering squad.

During this period, I achieved some successes. It was my information, for example, that helped put away an Italian gangster called Luigi Marotta. He had tried to defraud the

Ulster Bank in a £1.4 million scam using blank cheques from a liquor company based in Derry.

It felt good for a while. I was enjoying the work. But it wasn't the same as before. Sure, I was an agent of sorts, but I was no longer a soldier, and that hurt deeply. At the same time, I was consumed by bitterness at the way I had been treated. They – the British government, the Ministry of Defence, MI5, whoever it was that was responsible for paying me and arranging my relocation following the undercover work – still owed me. I had risked my life, after all, and I had saved lives. But at the heart of my predicament was the fact that I had been turned into a terrorist and got mixed up with murder and mayhem at the instigation of my handlers. No one was going to put their hands up to that.

As well as the anti-racketeering squad, I was also working for other agencies, among them the RUC's Criminal Investigation Department who assigned me handlers. They seemed happy with my pedigree and the extent of my contacts. They encouraged me to maintain and develop my contacts within the Real IRA, not least because its actions were at that time threatening to unravel the flimsy peace that existed in Northern Ireland.

On 12 August 1998, I drove to Dundalk for a meeting with a top IRA man, who I cannot name. I can't recall precisely, but I suspect I was simply thinking about my holiday. We were due to meet at midnight, a little dramatic perhaps, but the only time he could fit me in. Bang on time as always, I pulled up in the car park of the Claret Bar on the Crossmaglen Road and waited. His car eased into view a few minutes later and I got out of mine and into his. We were there to discuss a deal. He had asked me previously to provide guns for the Real IRA, but I needed more time and had called the meeting to tell him so. In the event, he didn't seem very interested in what I had to say. He was nervous, edgy and was clearly in a hurry.

But there was something else. Something unmistakable. I could see he had pink dust all over his pullover: it was fertiliser. There was something else too. When you make a bomb, the mix has a distinct, fusty, damp smell. It's usually accompanied by the smell of diesel. I could smell both of these distinct but unmistakable smells on him. There was no doubt in my mind that he had been making a bomb, and it struck me at the time that he must have broken off from mixing it to make the meeting.

'I can't be long,' he said. 'There's a big one on.'

I knew better than to ask him to elaborate, but it was clear something was imminent.

From my own experience, I knew that the time between making a bomb and detonating it is short. An assembled bomb retains its potency for a maximum of only seven days. Beyond that, the fertiliser becomes too caked and solid and has to be broken up.

The meeting with him lasted a few minutes. He was indeed in a hurry and darted off. I went home to bed and woke up early. I rang my handler, told him about the meeting and briefly outlined my concerns. We agreed that we needed to meet face to face – and quickly. By eleven o'clock, we were sitting at a quiet corner table at the Baytree Café in Holywood, east of Belfast, a place we had used before. We ordered coffee and cinnamon scones. I wasn't overly excited or dramatic. I was used to these meetings. I knew the score. I simply told him, clearly and concisely and without embellishment, everything I knew. I told him I believed something big was going down and told him exactly what was said at the meeting. I gave him the name of the man I had met – though he was aware of him and his status already – and his car registration number. I told him I didn't know where the bomb was going to go off or when, but I warned him the attack was imminent and explained about the fertiliser.

My handler, not one for theatrics, absorbed what I told him in a no-nonsense way. He pressed me for extra detail here and there, but was mainly content simply to sit and listen. I didn't need any reassurances that the kind of intelligence I was imparting would be given high priority. It wasn't my business, of course, but I imagined that it would be passed to those who needed to see it – to act upon it – immediately.

My wife and I flew to Tenerife the following morning and spent the rest of the day settling in to the hotel, exploring and enjoying the sunshine. But I found it hard to relax – I always do on holiday, and this time I had good reason. The next day, I awoke and began to dwell on what the man I had met had told me, turning over his words in my mind, analysing them, looking for hidden meaning in the nuances of our brief conversation. I was always like this when I picked up serious intelligence – I wasn't one simply to pass it on and forget about it. Later that day, I rang my father. Half of me believes, looking back, that I had some awful sixth sense about Omagh. The possibility of a bomb going off, and a big one, was definitely in the back of my mind somewhere. But the reality is that I simply rang the old fella to see if he was OK and to tell him about the holiday. I sat on the bed in my swimming trunks cradling the phone. Within seconds of the exchange of pleasantries, he delivered the savage news in his typical, unexcitable way. He told me that a car bomb had gone off in Omagh and that it had been a big one.

I said something like, 'You're joking.' Stupid thing to say. As if he would joke about a bomb.

'Honest to God, I'm watching the news and there are bodies everywhere,' came the reply.

This was it – the bomb I had told my RUC handler about. I felt the blind panic rise up inside me. I was only half-listening to the rest of what my father had to say. As soon as I got him off the line, I rang my handler. I remembered that he played football on a Saturday afternoon and expected his mobile to be switched off. But he answered it. I didn't have to say anything before he said, 'Kevin, I fucking know.'

'You did put that stuff in the system, didn't you?' I asked.

'Thank fuck I did,' was the reply.

So we had both done what we had to do, but it hadn't made any difference. I was devastated. What had happened to my information? How was it used? Was it used? Either way, there were, as my father said, bodies everywhere.

From my time in the IRA, I had become anaesthetised to all the bombs and killings, despite telling myself every day that I wasn't really part of it, that I was a soldier. I had become conditioned, programmed like a robot. Yet the Omagh atrocity took hold of you, grabbed you by the throat and made you try to understand. It brought all the madness into sharp focus and made you see it for what it was.

When I asked my handler about putting stuff in 'the system', I was referring to the RUC computer which logs and records information from handlers and agents. In theory, a sensitive report about an imminent terrorist attack would be sent to an intelligence analyst who would grade the information for its quality based on the reliability of the source, then forward it instantly to the army and MI5.

I have often been asked whether the man I informed on may have been making a bomb for somewhere else. But no other device went off before or after Omagh, and he is a known bomb-maker. I of all people knew that. I felt the security services or the RUC should have been watching him after my tip. He should have been put under twenty-four-hour surveillance to monitor whether anything was about to come over the border. That my information wasn't acted upon in any kind of satisfactory manner has provoked considerable debate, argument, claim and counter-claim. It has also caused the victims' families profound anguish. For my part, I am convinced that, if my information had been followed up, the Omagh atrocity could have been prevented.

In the past few years, I have talked to my handler a number of times about Omagh. I've asked him if he was sure he had put the information in the system. My handler was someone who did everything by the book. He said he put it in the system and I believe him. There is absolutely no doubt in my mind that he also believed the bomb that I told him about had been used at Omagh.

Three months after the atrocity I was watching TV at home. The police had got nowhere and Detective Chief Superintendent Eric Anderson, the man leading the investigation, was holding a press conference, begging for help to find the bombers. At one point, he appeared to break down. God knows what kind of strain he was under. The whole world, it seemed, was looking to him for answers, for justice. I felt sorry for him and something made me ring the inquiry headquarters. I'm not quite sure why I did it, as I had done what I had to do when I tipped off my handler. But something was troubling me – I needed to know what had happened to my intelligence after it was put into the system.

I arranged to meet Anderson at the Europa Hotel in Belfast the following day. We sat in the big first-floor bar overlooking the busy street below. I told him everything – my history, about how I had my meeting forty-eight hours before the bomb went off and about what he said. From his facial expressions, I could tell he seemed surprised. But, by nature a careful man, he didn't let his words betray him. He certainly gave the impression, however, that this was the first he had heard of my warning. Not for the first time, I felt physically sick.

At his request, I drove with Anderson and another detective across the border the following day to Carrickmacross in County Monaghan. The red Vauxhall Cavalier used by the terrorists which contained the bomb destined for Omagh was stolen from the town and I knew there was an IRA bomb-making factory in the area. I showed it to Anderson.

He turned to me as we were driving back and said,

'You know, this really is fantastic information. I can't thank you enough.'

What struck me as slightly odd at the time – but considerably less so now – was that I wasn't formally interviewed by a member of his team or asked to make a statement.

As the days went by, my concern about what I knew about Omagh abated slightly – only to resurface when the BBC programme *Panorama* broadcast its investigation into the bombing. Security sources gave the programme details of mobile-phone calls made to mobile phones used by the bombers in the Omagh area at the time of the explosion. Although the BBC did not know it, I knew that one of the numbers that made a call to one of the bomber's phones at the time of the attack was the number of the man I had met. I was able to identify it when a contact on the programme asked me for help, but the request came *after* the programme was screened. That man's call to one of the Omagh bombers lasted fifty-nine seconds.

So the man I knew was becoming something of a common thread, and I began to suspect that he was not quite what he seemed. He hadn't been pulled in for questioning over Omagh, an omission by the police and security services I found significant. That significance would magnify in the months and years to come. I learned later that he was never questioned about another murder. Was he, like me, a member of that rare protected species?

I decided then that his fate was inextricably linked to my own. I never stopped asking my handlers about him. Were they still pursuing that line of enquiry? Yes, of course, was the stock response. But nothing ever happened. He was never questioned and neither was I. Despite the pressure the police were under to get results, despite their countless appeals for even the tiniest scrap of intelligence, my comparatively sizeable nugget of information was being completely ignored.

But then something happened to change all that. A series of Sunday newspaper articles in Ireland in late 2000 blew my cover as a double agent within the IRA. To my horror, they detailed my work as a British agent both in the IRA and the RIRA. They didn't name me, of course, but they didn't need to. It would be obvious to the IRA. My cover had been blown. All those terrorists I had helped put in jail had been released under the Good Friday Agreement. Now they would realise it was me who got them caught. They were free but I wasn't.

My thoughts turned to my family: it would only be a matter of time before they learned about my double life. I decided I had better tell them the truth before they found out some other way. I started with my wife. One night around Christmas time, we sat watching a programme on the TV about undercover work. I blocked from my mind the knockout impact of what I was about to say, and just blurted it out. If I had thought too long about it, I don't think it would have trickled out the way it did.

'I'm one of them,' I said, without lifting my gaze from the TV. And then I told her I had been a double agent. For twenty years, she had known me as an IRA man. Now I was telling her that, well, I *was* an IRA man, but that I was really on the other side. The British side.

Gradually, I unloaded my story – not every detail, that

would have to wait, but the bare bones, enough eventually to convince her. I felt no sense of relief. I just delivered what I had to say as if being debriefed. Naturally – and I was expecting this – my wife's incredulity gave way to fear. Her old man was a tout. He would end up dead. I told her I would go on the run and explained how I had been let down over my money and relocation and a new identity. I promised I would never give up fighting for what I was owed, what we were both owed and what we need to survive. I told her she had nothing to fear and that, whatever the IRA was, it wouldn't allow her to be harmed. She had done nothing wrong. But she would have to face everyone – family, friends, workmates, shopkeepers, you name it. There would be those who would deliver direct insults, spit in her face with as much vitriol as they could muster. And there would be the less direct taunts, the darkly muttered name-calling from passers-by. People in Newry could handle my being in the Provisional IRA. What they couldn't tolerate was the fact that I really worked for the other side. She would have to face all that, and so would our families.

It should never have come to this, I thought, as I saw her looking at me as though I should be pitied rather than censured. God bless her. She was angry too, though. I was a fool, she said, for believing that they – the Brits – would look after me. She said she would stay behind, and bravely calculating that at most our windows would be done in – which as it transpired they were – she accepted my assurance that she would never be harmed.

Being in the IRA meant risking your life and liberty

practically every day – putting your loved ones through hell. That was what she had been forced to deal with in the past. But this – being exposed as a double agent, or informant, or tout, whatever you want to call it – meant only one thing: certain death. And, no doubt, a grisly, unspeakable one at that.

I had spent the past twenty years in a near-constant state of anxiety, but with my cover blown – and without the safety net of relocation – I would be looking over my shoulder until the day I died, which I have always believed will be sooner rather than later. They will undoubtedly get me. It may sound fatalistic, but that is just the way it is. It might suit the IRA to let me live now, while I'm still a living embarrassment to the British government, spilling details about handlers and the security services and so on. But they'll get me in the end.

The death threats came from the IRA and RIRA sure enough, but by then I was already on the run in England. A dead man walking. Through a variety of means, I joined forces with others who had worked, at some point in their lives, for army intelligence but who, like me, had been stitched up. Hearing their tales gave me some kind of comfort, but their stories paled and seemed almost insignificant when held up to mine.

I decided that I would go public. I had nothing else to lose. Besides, there was Omagh to think about. What I told my handler about the top Real IRA man I had met was still troubling me. Nothing had been done about it, I was sure of that.

When the stories broke about the intelligence I had given

forty-eight hours before Omagh, there was an almighty outcry. They brought worldwide attention. Politicians, police and the security services went into a spin. The victims' families felt understandable confusion and anger.

I waited for the inevitable backlash, and it came. First in with the boot was RUC chief constable Sir Ronnie Flanagan, who denounced me as a 'Walter Mitty' character. He was followed by people in the security services who did everything they could to discredit me, passing me off as a fantasist who at best only ever supplied low-grade information. It didn't take much to understand why they were so keen to rubbish me. I was damaging them, embarrassing them.

I knew that by speaking out I would make enemies; I knew that plenty of people would be more inclined to believe, in many cases unquestioningly, the likes of Flanagan than me. But there is a saying that I have always followed and it is this: 'Lord help me keep my big mouth shut until I know what I'm talking about.' I stick by that. I was telling the truth.

In my darkest moments, and there were more than a few, I sometimes wavered and wondered privately whether I was doing the right thing. I always concluded that there was no other course of action open to me. For all those who tried to dismiss me, there were many, many more who supported me. People in the army, the police and the security services privately urged me to keep going. They know how important it is for the truth to win out. I resolved to plough on and keep talking.

Finally, late in 2001, there was a breakthrough. The police ombudsman in Northern Ireland announced that it would look into my claims and launch an investigation. The RUC was plainly horrified, and saw it as a direct challenge to its power. It felt quickly obliged to scotch any suggestions that it had failed to act properly. No doubt, the security services were aghast too. Inevitably, the ombudsman would be shining light on areas that many would rather remain in darkness, not least the sticky issue of agents and their handlers. However, the relatives of the bomb victims welcomed the development, believing that the allegations were too serious to be left to hang in the air.

Maybe it was the cynic in me, but I suspected that the police ombudsman, Nuala O'Loan, would produce a whitewash. I could not have been more wrong. The report was savage, damning stuff. It was highly critical of senior officers, including Sir Ronnie Flanagan, and of Special Branch for failing to act on information. The report centred on my allegations, but also uncovered a second warning of an attack in Omagh on 15 August, the day of the bombing. It listed a catalogue of serious flaws in the original investigation and recommended the appointment of an independent senior officer to head the bomb probe, and a review of the role of Special Branch.

Mrs O'Loan directed her criticism at Sir Ronnie Flanagan and other senior officers over the 'defective leadership, poor judgement and lack of urgency' with the inquiry. 'As a result of that, the chances of detaining and convicting the Omagh bombers have been significantly reduced,' she said. 'There was a terrible atrocity in Omagh on 15 August 1998. We have to look at why that investigation has not been properly conducted. We have established facts which indicated that one of the problems is the fact that intelligence is not disseminated in an appropriate way by Special Branch.'

The report fell short of saying the RUC could have prevented the bombing, but in a reference to the anonymous call received in addition to my tip-off it concluded, 'It will never be known whether or not the bombing of Omagh could have been prevented if the RUC had taken more action in relation to the information it received during the period between 4 and 15 August 1998.'

I noted with amazement that no record of my meeting with my handler 'could be found in Special Branch' despite claims that the information was passed on.

There was something else, something deeply significant. The man I had met was named as 'A' in the report which said that the 'role of A was not fully investigated, despite the alleged telephone call made from A's mobile phone on the day of the bombing.'

It confirmed my suspicions that he, too, was a double agent.

It was the detail about Omagh in the report and the information I provided that legitimised my case. At least, that's how I saw it. This is what the report said: 'Three days before the bombing of Omagh, the RUC also received information from a "reliable" informant known as Kevin Fulton, which indicated that terrorists were about to "move something north over the next few days".'

It added:

'If the Fulton intelligence had been considered along with other material held, had been properly assessed and documented, before deciding on no action, then the action of Special Branch might have been defensible. Regrettably, the intelligence was not assessed or considered. A consideration of the intelligence may have resulted in the following action: Fulton could have been instructed by his RUC handler to find out more information, if possible enquiries could have been made by An Garda Siochana to establish whether they had any relevant information. Border surveillance units could have been alerted to take note of the movements of 'A' and his vehicle. Some covert policing may have been possible. Kevin Fulton was, and has been, a source of significant information and intelligence in the past. His grading as an informant in and around the time of the Omagh bomb consistently reflects the fact that he was regarded as "reliable". No evidence has been found to justify the contention that he was regarded by the RUC at the time of the Omagh bomb as unreliable.

Between June 1998 and August 1998 Kevin Fulton was graded as an "A1" by CID. "A1" infers that the source is 'reliable' and the information "accurate".

During this time Special Branch gave Fulton's information a grading of "B2" which inferred the source is "usually reliable" and the information is "believed accurate". In July 1997 Kevin Fulton was granted "participating informant" status by the assistant chief constable crime. This means he was authorised by that senior officer to take part in a crime in order to enable the police to prevent a serious crime, or if it did take place, to arrest the principal offenders. Throughout his involvement with the RUC, Fulton received substantial financial rewards from the RUC and from other organisations. The police ombudsman was informed by senior Special Branch officers that on one occasion Fulton provided information which led to the prevention of a very serious attack and "he undoubtedly saved lives"'.

The ombudsman's report then details the measures taken to discredit me, which began some 18 months after the Omagh bombing. The report said:

'On May 10 2000 Fulton was declared "dangerous" as a CID source, and he was documented as being 'unreliable' after articles appeared in newspapers referring to an "RUC mole" and it was thought by Special Branch that Fulton had inspired them. On August 21 2001 Kevin Fulton was described by the head of the Special Branch to the police ombudsman's office as "an intelligence nuisance"'.

Walter Mitty? An intelligence nuisance? The police ombudsman didn't seem to think so. And neither did the families of the bomb victims, some of whom I have got to know well. Michael Gallagher, whose son Adrian was killed in the blast, said that, if this was America and I had infiltrated Al Qaeda and not the IRA, I would be a national hero for what I had done. I don't want to be a national hero, but I gratefully accept the point he was making. He also said this:

'Sir Ronnie Flanagan called him a Walter Mitty but, when Nuala O'Loan published her report, it emerged that he had been a very credible agent. I noted recently that Tom Kelly, the

Downing Street press officer who called the weapons
inspector Dr David Kelly a Walter Mitty, was also Tony Blair's
right-hand man at the time of the Omagh bomb.

I found it interesting to note that connection, and that three
years ago, when the authorities wanted to discredit Kevin
Fulton over Omagh, they called him a Walter Mitty. That's the
tag for anyone who challenges the system.

I also think it is absurd for someone like Ronnie Flanagan
or anyone in the security services to say that Kevin Fulton
is a liar.

This is a man who survived by telling lies and was trained
and asked to do so by the security services.

Yet, to call him a liar now after the internal assessments that
I know the ombudsman saw, which verified his standing as a
highly reliable intelligence source, is sending a very bad
message to other people who may want to work for the
security services but see how he has been treated.

The intelligence services do not want to recognise Kevin
because that would mean admitting the underhand way in
which their system works.'

Others, including the former army intelligence officer
Martin Ingram, have since come forward publicly to vouch
for me, which has helped my cause immensely. A former
RUC officer in Newry has verified my standing as a leading
IRA man in the town. The officer – who had no objection to
his own background being checked – said, 'I knew Kevin
Fulton and had many, many run-ins with him. I knew him
as a leading IRA man in the Newry area in the 1980s and

1990s. But later I discovered he was working for the security services. I couldn't believe it, to be honest. He moved with the top boys down there and we pulled him in on many occasions. I never suspected at first that he was anything other than an IRA man. He played his role brilliantly. I've got to give him that. None of us had any idea whatsoever that he was a British agent.'

The officer said it was around 1993 when he realised that I was working for British intelligence – after an incident in Hillsborough, County Down. 'A church minister was out walking his dog early one morning in Hillsborough when he saw what he thought was suspicious activity. A man was with another group of men, exchanging something or dropping something off.

'The minister took down the registration numbers of both vehicles. We recognised one car immediately as being Fulton's and caught up with him at a petrol station and took him to the Maze search centre. We held him for hours while the matter was looked into.

'We discovered that there were no details in the computer of the vehicle registration of the other car seen at the secret rendezvous. That could mean only one thing. The car belonged to some branch of the security services. It was obvious he'd been meeting with Special Branch or MI5 or someone. We let Fulton go.

'A lot of things from the past suddenly started to fall into place. We knew he was up to all sorts in Newry but nothing ever stuck. It was then I knew why – he was an agent.'

In a further twist, one of my handlers is prepared to testify in court on my behalf. He is prepared to become the first army or police handler in the history of the Troubles to break the Official Secrets Act and blow the activities of the undercover services in Ulster wide open.

The ex-handler, who cannot be named for security reasons, praised my ability for working undercover. 'He was never a Walter Mitty character. He's a fascinating character, for sure, but he was a valuable agent who took risks to get the information we needed. I feel honour-bound to speak up on his behalf. He saved lives and took risks. I wasn't surprised to learn about Omagh. The security services missed out on plenty of "results" against terrorism because it failed to act on Fulton's information.'

But I was particularly touched by what Michael Gallagher said when interviewed by the *Belfast Newsletter*. He also said he was grateful to me for instigating the ombudsman's inquiry. We were both battling for justice and our paths had crossed along our respective journeys. We had been able to help each other and that felt good.

Mr Gallagher knew my suspicions and, like me, he wanted to know why the senior IRA man I'd warned my handler about two days prior to the Omagh bombing hadn't been questioned about Omagh. In January 2002, the matter was raised publicly. Under legal privilege provided by parliament, Jeffrey Donaldson MP named in the House of Commons the Omagh bomb-maker.

He was the man referred to in the police ombudsman's report as 'A'.

The man has never publicly replied to this allegation.

According to the ombudsman's report, 'A"s mobile phone was also traced to a call to the Real IRA Omagh bomb convoy on its way to the Tyrone town on the day of the atrocity. Yet the RUC chief constable Sir Ronnie Flanagan has publicly and confidently stated that 'A' never has and never will be a suspect in the bombing.

Why not? Is it because he was a secret agent? He has never been questioned about the Colleen McMurray murder either. Was he – is he – being protected as I once was?

If that is the case, it is hard to see the families of the bomb victims ever discovering the truth or seeing justice done.

I began what I described as a legal battle to save my life. The Belfast High Court granted me leave to seek a judicial review of the decision by the Northern Ireland Office not to give me protection. Justice Brian Kerr dismissed claims by lawyers acting for the government that some of the grounds on which I was seeking the review were insufficient. At the heart of my case is my contention that I was promised by my British intelligence handlers that I would be taken care of with a new identity and a financial package if my cover was ever blown.

Government barrister Declan Morgan QC tried to argue that the handlers were not properly identified in my legal team's initial submission to the court.

True. But normal rules didn't apply in the intelligence world. My team said handlers were often only known by first names which were themselves false.

Justice Kerr said, 'If a person is told by two Special Branch officers that he is going to be looked after when he stops informing, does that not afford him a legitimate expectation that that will be the case?'

The judge's decision was a breakthrough, but I have a long way to go and there are plenty of people who want me stopped. I have had my home in London raided and burgled twice. My phone has been bugged. No paperwork exists about my work for the security services.

In the meantime, I am living in London in limbo. I can't sign on the dole for fear of being traced or killed. The Northern Ireland Office did move me into a flat, but it later sent me a letter saying it had decided that I could live safely in Britain without a new identity. It was just another brush off, another way of washing their hands of me.

If I stay in England, I will have to live under my real name. Kevin Fulton is a pseudonym, a cover name. It provides the thinnest veil of protection. Under my real name, I could easily be tracked down and killed by any one of the terrorists I betrayed over fifteen years. Mind you, as the grisly fate of other IRA enemies has shown us, they can get you anywhere, any time, if they know who you are.

The fact is I'm not supposed to be here. I have no doubt I was supposed to have died years ago, like many other agents. I was close to it, but I saw it coming and got out. How many other agents didn't get out in time? It is highly unlikely we will ever know.

Last year I found out just how close I came to death. The man who had interrogated me twice over Martindale was uncovered as a double agent. I sensed he was desperate to nail me. His exposure as a tout for the British makes it clear why he wanted me dead.

He knew that outing me as a tout would leave him free to carry on his work without suspicion. The Provisional IRA would be satisfied that the mole within the organisation had been smoked out, leaving him free to carry on his dubious work with impunity. He wanted me dead, and my handlers counted on him killing me. That's why they wanted me to go back to the third interrogation into the Martindale operation. They knew I had been compromised, and I was of no use to them any more. They counted on him stiffing me, thus saving them from having to honour their promise to me of a new life if it all went wrong.

EPILOGUE

Just weeks after this book was published in June 2006, plain-clothes officers from the Police Service of Northern Ireland (PSNI) raided my 'secret' address in the UK, the offices of the book's publisher, John Blake and the homes of the book's ghost writers, Jim Nally and Ian Gallagher. The PSNI officers – who stated they were investigating unsolved murders referred to in this book – seized documents, audio tapes and computer hard drives from all four addresses.

On 1 November 2006, I was arrested in southern England and flown to Belfast for questioning. I was held for five days. During that time, officers from C2 serious crime unit questioned me 30 times about the unsolved murders of Eoin Morley, British soldier Cyril Smith and RUC officer Colleen McMurray.

I had hoped that my admissions in this book would create

a stir. In truth, though, I expected the security services and the intelligence agencies to react as they usually react to damaging revelations – to ignore them. I expected them to issue a firm 'no comment', while briefing their slavish coterie of 'security' and 'home affairs' journalists to the effect that I'm not credible.

Instead, by arresting me on suspicion of murder, the PSNI unwittingly confirmed that what I say is true. It soon became clear, however, that the PSNI's motive in arresting me wasn't to confirm my claims in this book, but to protect themselves on a different front.

Weeks after the book was published in 2006, I was contacted by the defence team of the man accused of carrying out the Omagh bombing in August 1998. They wanted to know if I would be willing to give evidence at his trial. Sean Hoey, a 38-year-old electrician from South Armagh, faced 56 charges relating to the Real IRA bombing of Omagh on 15 August, 1998 which killed 29 people.

Of course, I want the world to know what I know about Omagh. That's why I've gone public about the information I passed on to the security services days before the atrocity was carried out. That's why I've gone public about the man I believed carried out this attack. If cross-examined by Hoey's team about what I knew in relation to the Omagh attack, I would tell the truth. The security services in Northern Ireland couldn't take that chance. By arresting me for offences referred to in this book, the PSNI was making one point abundantly clear: if I were to confess to crimes in open court during the trial of Sean Hoey, they would charge me over those crimes. In other words, by giving evidence at Hoey's trial and admitting my part in certain crimes, I would be incriminating myself. This put me in a dreadful bind. Mercifully, in the end, I wasn't called. I found out why at the end of Hoey's trial – the case against him was so weak scientifically that his defence team didn't need to cross-examine the likes of me to get their client cleared.

Sure enough, on 20 December 2007, after a trial at Belfast High Court lasting 56 days, Hoey was found not guilty of all charges relating to the Omagh bombing. Justice Weir at Belfast Crown Court said police were guilty of a 'deliberate and calculated deception' in their handling of the investigation. He criticised the 'slapdash approach' taken by the police to some of the evidence, and accused two officers of telling untruths to the court which made their testimony invalid.

In the absence of eyewitness accounts or intelligence-based evidence, the prosecution relied on a new forensic technique known as low copy number DNA (LCN DNA). This involves using just a few samples with only a few cells to obtain a DNA profile of a suspect. The court was told that the molecules used in this process are the size of a millionth of a grain of salt. However, during the trial, expert after expert attacked the process. UK forensic scientist Professor Allan Jamieson, told the court that LCN DNA was unreliable and that the tests were open to interpretation.

When Hoey walked free, the victims' families were, unsurprisingly, furious. Michael Gallagher, whose son Aidan died in the bombing, said, 'I think it is beyond belief what we have had to put up with over the last nine-and-a-half years.'

He added, 'There will be at least ten people who will be sitting at their Christmas dinner this year who were involved in the Omagh bomb.' He said intelligence agencies knew who the people were. The fact is, I know who these people are. 'We have to face hard facts, the victims of the Omagh bomb will receive no justice. It's depressing but true and part of the reason for that is the presence of so many informers in this plot.'

To this day, I've never been questioned by police about the Omagh bombing.

The families are calling for a cross-border public enquiry into the atrocity – and they have received support from an unlikely source – Hoey's mother. 'I want to ask the question regarding the Omagh tragedy – who has the most to fear from such an enquiry? What are the authorities north and south trying to cover up?'

Of course, the public enquiry will never happen. Too many people in too many top positions have too much to hide.

In my opinion, the whole Omagh non-investigation is a cover-up, orchestrated at the highest levels of the police and the intelligence services. However, it comes as no surprise to me that the people who run these agencies could be capable of such actions to safeguard their careers and their reputations.

Indeed, I am now of the opinion that perfecting the art of shafting those below you while feathering your own nest is a prerequisite skill if you want to scale the intelligence ladder.

After eleven years working for MI5, Bob was sent to Northern Ireland in the late eighties to assist the Force

Research Unit (FRU), the army's undercover force responsible for infiltrating Irish terror groups. It was Bob who met me in New York when I purchased infra-red detonation equipment for the IRA. It was Bob who debriefed me in March 1992 about the IRA's use of flashgun technology to detonate bombs – just hours before this very technology was used to murder RUC officer Colleen McMurray. It was Bob who repeatedly promised me a new identity and a new life if my role as a British double agent was ever exposed to the IRA.

Currently, I am taking my former employer, the British State, to court. I've launched a civil action, in which I'm seeking only what I'd been constantly promised by handlers like Bob – a new identity and a pay-off.

Already, a number of courageous FRU members have pledged to give evidence corroborating my claims. The Judge has ruled that I can call any witness who can provide evidence as to my value as an undercover agent.

But first I have to make it to court. My case against the British State has been dragging on for five years now, with no sign of it actually coming to court. If you think spying is the most duplicitous, immoral and dirty game in town, then you haven't encountered our wonderful legal system. My nemesis, the British State, has tirelessly exploited every conceivable legal loophole to obstruct and thwart the process. Clearly, someone in power thinks they can starve me or bore me into giving up. Or maybe they're counting on some sort of third party intervention to make me go away. After all, every day that I am denied my due is another day when I could get whacked – and that would suit them fine.

It sounds melodramatic, until you consider the fate of other men who've served as double agents for the British in Northern Ireland. Take Sinn Fein party official Denis Donaldson. On 4 April 2006, Donaldson was found shot dead inside a remote cottage in County Donegal. Donaldson had taken refuge here after his exposure as a British spy five months earlier, in December 2005.

Donaldson's murder scared me because, like me, he'd been hung out to dry by his former employers at MI5 and Special Branch. Donaldson's murder scared me because, like me, once his usefulness ran out he was abandoned and left for dead. I believe that whoever set Donaldson up to be murdered could do the same to me any minute of any day. Donaldson's murder made me realise just how dispensable we agents are, now that we're no longer of any value to the intelligence services.

Donaldson's career in the IRA and Sinn Fein spanned the entirety of the Troubles – from the rebirth of the IRA in 1970 to Sinn Fein's growth into Northern Ireland's largest nationalist party. He was from old Republican stock, and had been party to crucial events in Republican history. In 1970, he was fêted as a hero for defending the vulnerable Catholic communities in the Short Strand district of Belfast against loyalist attacks. When he served time in Long Kesh for terrorist offences, he became close friends with IRA icon Bobby Sands.

Later, Donaldson travelled the world for the IRA, visiting Europe and many parts of the Middle East. In Lebanon, he was closely involved in negotiations to secure the release of Belfast-born hostage Brian Keenan. He was also sent to the

KEVIN FULTON

United States, where he served as a contact point with the crucial Irish-American community. Through all his international travels in the eighties, Donaldson's role was symbolic of Sinn Fein's 'ballot box in one hand, a hand grenade in the other' hypocrisy. Outwardly, he sought legitimate political support; secretly he procured weapons and finance to help the IRA continue 'the armed struggle'.

Incredibly, all this time, he was supplying MI5 and RUC Special Branch with intelligence. His information helped the British authorities strangle the supply of crucial aid from the United States and to intercept arms shipments from the Middle East. Donaldson maintained his cover because no-one in the IRA dared question a man so imbued with Republican credibility. That said, for every minute of every day of all those years, Donaldson must have lived by the seat of his pants just as I had done. Every time he walked out of his front door, he must have dreaded 'a tug' from an armed stranger or a bullet in his head. Every time the doorbell rang or someone called his name in the street, he must have wondered, 'Is this it? Has the time come?'

When the Good Friday Agreement held and democratic power-sharing returned to Northern Ireland in the late nineties, Donaldson must have thought he'd run his race. Then, in 2000, he became a vital cog in Sinn Fein's political machine, and his double life resumed. I believe that once they've got you, the spooks, they don't let go until they've squeezed every last calorie of use out of you. They're a bit like the people they're supposed to be fighting, the terrorists, in that way. Donaldson was appointed Sinn Fein party office administrator. For MI5, this meant it had someone inside the very heart of an organisation it still deeply distrusted.

Then came his bizarre unmasking as a spy – and his death sentence. In October 2002, he was arrested in a raid on the Sinn Fein offices as part of a high-profile police investigation into an alleged Irish republican spy ring – an affair known as Stormontgate. The police accused Donaldson and others of amassing large amounts of confidential documents from both the Northern Ireland office and from local political parties. The implication was that this confidential information could be used by Sinn Fein to smear or intimidate political rivals. To the outside world, it appeared that Sinn Fein had failed to give up its old terrorist tricks.

These raids brought down the power-sharing agreement. Northern Ireland's uncomfortable peace fidgeted ominously.

It turns out that the IRA – oblivious to the fact that Donaldson was spying on them for the British – had ordered Donaldson to start spying on political opponents at Stormont. He was instructed to co-ordinate the collection and photo-copying of confidential documents - something he had been doing for British intelligence for almost two decades. In other words, the IRA ordered the British spy to start spying on the British.

Then, Donaldson was exposed as being a double agent. In December 2005, the Public Prosecution Service for Northern Ireland dropped the spy-ring charges against Donaldson and two other men on the grounds that it would not be in the 'public interest' to proceed with the case. On 16 December 2005, Sinn Fein President Gerry Adams announced to a press conference in Dublin that Donaldson had been a spy in the pay of British intelligence. Donaldson confirmed this in a statement to RTE, the Irish state broadcaster. It was what Donaldson didn't say that pricked my interest.

Donaldson said he was recruited after 'compromising himself' during a 'vulnerable' time in his life. He didn't specify why he was vulnerable or how this resulted in him 'turning'. I know from my days as an agent that the usual methods include entrapment, assistance with criminal charges, financial inducement or – if all else fails – blackmail. One of my former handlers tells me a story involving Donaldson and a woman who was married to a senior figure in the IRA. He insists that this relationship proved pivotal to Donaldson's decision to risk his life and become a British mole.

What really intrigues me, though, is who would have benefited from Donaldson's murder. Not Sinn Fein. Sure, the old procedure would have been to dispatch Donaldson with a bullet to the back of the head. The IRA murdered at least 50 people it alleged worked as 'touts' for the police or British intelligence. But for Sinn Fein in 2005, whacking Donaldson would have made a mockery of their solemn and historic pronouncements about decommissioning and the move away from terrorism towards democratic politics. Besides, the hierarchy had allowed him to go free, in disgrace. Donaldson himself believed this. That is why he relocated to an old derelict family holiday home just a few miles across the border. If he thought his life was in danger, surely Donaldson would have done what I have done and fled abroad?

The general public had no idea where Donaldson was hiding until 19 March 2006. On that date, Dublin-based weekly tabloid *The Sunday World* published a story by journalist Hugh Jordan revealing the whereabouts of Donaldson's hideout – a ramshackle cottage without electricity or running water in the remote townland of Classey, 5 miles from the tiny village of Glenties on the road to Doochary in Donegal. This is truly the middle of nowhere. Less than three weeks later, Donaldson was dead.

The last person Donaldson spoke to – apart from his killers – is Tom Cranley, a census taker who chatted to him at the cottage at about 8.30pm the previous evening. His body was found by Gardai at about 5pm the next day after a passer-by reported seeing a broken window and a smashed-in door.

Two shotgun cartridges were found at the threshold of the cottage. Two shots had been fired through the front door, apparently as he attempted to bolt it. Another two cartridges hit him as he fled inside. A post-mortem revealed he died from a shotgun blast to the chest. His right hand was badly damaged by the other gunshot. Donaldson died in his pyjamas.

On 8 April 2006, Donaldson was buried in Belfast City Cemetery, rather than at the republican Milltown Cemetery. The provisional IRA issued a one-line statement saying that it had 'no involvement whatsoever' in the murder. Could Donaldson's murderer have worked for someone else? Was Donaldson sacrificed to protect other agents implanted at even more strategic levels within Sinn Fein? It seems to me that this is becoming a familiar pattern.

KEVIN FULTON

In February 2008, MI5 took one of Gerry Adams' personal drivers into protective custody when he too was unmasked as a British agent. MI5 advised Roy McShane to leave his west Belfast home after it emerged that an internal IRA investigation found he had been working for the British for more than a decade.

McShane was one of a pool of drivers working for leading members of Sinn Fein since the first ceasefire of 1994. He drove Gerry Adams, the Sinn Fein President, during the run-up to the Good Friday Agreement in 1998, one of the most crucial periods of the Irish peace process.

McShane is understood to have worked as a pool driver for Adams at the same time that the security services were bugging a car which transported Martin McGuinness to and from negotiations. The late Mo Mowlam, then Northern Ireland secretary, had authorised the bugging of a car driven by an IRA intelligence officer throughout 1997 and '98.

I have no doubt that the identity of more 'British moles' who were embedded in the highest echelons of the IRA and Sinn Fein will emerge. Each unmasking of a double agent, tout or grass begs the same old question – who was running this murky, dirty war in Northern Ireland?

It was a Dirty War, and I was treated like dirt. But I won't stand for it.

All I want is for my government to do right by me. If they don't, then I will keep talking and fighting until I die. That's the way it is.

I was among the spectators at the Remembrance Day parade in Whitehall in November. I stood there, closed my

eyes and remembered colleagues in the Royal Irish Rangers –
my regiment – who were killed by the IRA. Later, I laid a
poppy cross in the regimental plot at the Garden of
Remembrance at Westminster Abbey.

I can't take part in the parade itself. I can't march shoulder
to shoulder with the men from the Rangers because the
Ministry of Defence refuses to recognise my service as a soldier.

But that's all I ever was. A soldier.